Motion to Terminate Based on Vacated Conviction

Example Showing How to Get Your Deportation Reversed Due to Successful Criminal Relief

Attorney Brian D. Lerner

LAW OFFICES OF
BRIAN D. LERNER
A PROFESSIONAL CORPORATION

ATTORNEY DRAFTED IMMIGRATION PETITIONS

By

Brian D. Lerner

Attorney at Law

Disclaimer and Terms of Use:

INTRODUCTION

There are a multitude of different immigration petitions and applications. They are complex and full of requirements. Obviously, it would be best to hire an immigration attorney to best prepare the petitions and applications. However, this can certainly cost thousands of dollars.

The next best option is to get a sample of the petition written by an experienced immigration attorney. The samples cost a fraction what would be charged by an immigration attorney. However, while the reader has to alter, amend and change the parts of the sample petition to reflect their actual situation, it is a fantastic roadmap for them to use. If the reader has purchased the entire petition or application, they will have real live samples of cover letters, forms, declarations, affidavits and the necessary exhibits to use. The samples come from real cases and the names of those clients have been redacted to protect the privacy of that person or corporation.

These are petitions and applications that have been drafted by an experienced immigration attorney with over 25 years of experience. Get the benefits of that experience without the costs.

CONTENTS

About the Law Offices of Brian D. Lerner

Brian D. Lerner has been a licensed attorney since 1992 and started the Law Offices of Brian D. Lerner, APC. The law practice consists of Immigration and Nationality Law and everything involved with and regarding immigration which includes citizenship, investment visas, family and employment visas, removal and deportation hearings, appeals, waivers, adjustment, consulate processing and all types of immigration and citizenship matters. Thousands of families have been reunited and/or permitted to stay in the U.S. and/or return to the U.S. because of the successful work of Immigration Attorney Brian D. Lerner

This law offices handles all types of immigration cases including family based and employment based. Immigration issues range from immigration court proceedings to trying to fix what paralegals may have done that was neither correct nor proper. Foreign nationals must have experience lawyers admitted to practice law.

The Law Offices of Brian D. Lerner, APC, handles cases arising from business visas, work permits, Green Cards, non-immigrant visas, deportation, citizenship, appeals and all areas of immigration. The Law Offices of Brian D. Lerner, APC does EB-5 Investor Visas, H-1B Specialty Occupation, L-1 Intracompany Transferee, E-2 Treaty Investor, E-1 Treaty Trader, O-1 Extraordinary Ability among others. Regarding immigrant visas for the Green Card, the firm does PERM and advanced degree PERM, Family Petitions, and Extraordinary Alien Petitions. In addition to affirmative petitions, the Law Firm represents people in people in deportation and removal hearings, including political asylum, withholding of removal, and convention against torture cases.

Brian D. Lerner has been certified as an expert in Immigration & Nationality Law by the California State Bar, Board of Legal Specialization since 2000 and has been re-certified three times. He now passes on his decades of experience by allowing the Reader, Law Schools, Professors and other Immigration Attorneys to purchase sample petitions on every facet of Immigration Law.

About Motion to Reopen Removal Proceedings – Vacated Conviction

An order of removal. If a criminal conviction is vacated or reduced, it allows that person to go back to immigration court and try to either get the deportation order reversed or to become eligible for relief that did not exist prior to the crime being vacated.

MOTION TO REOPEN AND TERMINATE REMOVAL PROCEEDINGS

Brian D. Lerner (Bar No. 158536)
Christopher A. Reed (Bar No. 235438)
Law Offices of Brian D. Lerner, APC
3233 E. Broadway
Long Beach, California 90803
Telephone: (562) 495-0554
Facsimile: (562) 608-8672

Attorneys for Respondent

UNITED STATES DEPARTMENT OF JUSTICE

EXECUTIVE OFFICE FOR IMMIGRATION REVIEW

IMMIGRATION COURT

LOS ANGELES, CALIFORNIA

In the Matter of:

███████████

Respondent,

In Removal Proceedings.

File No: ███████████

Immigration Judge: Kevin W. Riley   Next Hearing: N/A

MOTION TO REOPEN AND TERMINATE REMOVAL PROCEEDINGS BASED ON CONVICTIONS VACATED PURSUANT TO SECTION 1473.7 OF THE CALIFORNIA PENAL CODE

TABLE OF CONTENTS

Brian D. Lerner (Bar No. 158536)
Christopher A. Reed (Bar No. 235438)
Law Offices of Brian D. Lerner, APC
3233 E. Broadway
Long Beach, California 90803
Telephone: (562) 495-0554
Facsimile: (562) 608-8672

Attorneys for Respondent

UNITED STATES DEPARTMENT OF JUSTICE

EXECUTIVE OFFICE FOR IMMIGRATION REVIEW

IMMIGRATION COURT

LOS ANGELES, CALIFORNIA

In the Matter of:

███████████████████

Respondent,

In Removal Proceedings.

File No: A███████████

Pursuant to section 240(c)(7) of the Immigration and Nationality Act (hereinafter "INA" or "Act") and 8 C.F.R. § 1003.23(b)(1), Respondent, through undersigned counsel, moves the Immigration Court to reopen and terminate his removal proceedings given that his two underlying convictions have been vacated pursuant to section 1473.7 of the California Penal Code and therefore, that he is no longer removable from the United States as charged.

\

I.
JURISDICTION AND VENUE

Subject to certain exceptions, pursuant to INA § 240(c)(7), an alien may file only one motion to reopen, which must be filed within 90 days of the date of entry of a final administrative order of removal. *See also* 8 C.F.R. § 1003.23(b)(1).

However, an Immigration Judge may also upon his or her own motion "at any time" reopen or reconsider any case in which he or she has made a decision, unless jurisdiction is vested with the Board of Immigration Appeals (hereinafter "BIA" or "Board"). *Id.; see also Matter of J-J-*, 21 I&N Dec. 976 (BIA 1997).

A motion to reopen should be filed with the Immigration Court having administrative control over the Record of Proceedings. *Id.* at § 1003.23(b)(1)(ii). Typically, this is where the in order of removal or deportation was entered. In the present case, Respondent was ordered removed by the Immigration Court in Los Angeles, California. Therefore, Respondent's motion is properly before this Court.

II.
STATEMENT OF RELEVANT FACTS

1. Respondent is a 42-year-old male, native and citizen of Iran. Tabs A-B and H.

2. Respondent was admitted to the United States as a Lawful Permanent Resident at Los Angles, California on or about August 29, 1991. Tabs A and H.

3. Respondent's mother is a Naturalized Citizen of the United States. Tab C.

4. On December 2, 2004, Respondent was convicted of Possession of a Controlled Substance (Methamphetamine) in violation of section 11377(a) of the California Health and Safety Code. Tab F.

5.   On December 11, 2007, Respondent was convicted of Identity Theft in violation of section 530.5(a) of the California Penal Code and sentenced to two years state prison. Tab G.

6.   As a result of the above convictions, the Department of Homeland Security (hereinafter "DHS") initiated removal proceedings against Respondent in 2011 with service of a Notice to Appear, charging him with removability under section 237(a)(2)(A)(iii) of the Act, as an alien convicted of an aggravated felony, as defined in section 101(a)(43)(G) of the Act (theft or burglary offense with a term of imprisonment of at least 1 year) and 237(a)(2)(B)(i) of the Act, as an alien convicted of violating a law or regulation relating to a controlled substance, as defined in section 102 of the Controlled Substance Act, 21 USC § 802. Tab H.

7.   On October 17, 2011, Respondent was ordered removed from the United States to Iran.

8.   Respondent remains inside the United States under an Order of Supervision and has been reporting with Immigration and Customs Enforcement (hereinafter "ICE") without incident since February 6, 2012. Tab I.

9.   On November 30, 2018, Respondent's 2004 and 2007 convictions were vacated pursuant to section 1473.7 of the California Penal Code and the charges against him were dismissed. Tabs F-G.

III.
ARGUMENT.

A.   **Respondent is No Longer Removable from the United States As Charged and Therefore, This Court Should Reopen and Terminate His Removal Proceedings.**

In the present case, the two charges of removability against Respondent (INA § 237(a)(2)(A)(iii) and INA § 237(a)(2)(B)(i)) were based on his 2004 possession conviction and his 2007 identify theft conviction. Tab G. However, as explained above, those convictions have since been vacated pursuant to section 1473.7(a) of the California Penal Code, which allows for a motion to vacate if: (1) a conviction or sentence is legally invalid due to a prejudicial error damaging the moving party's ability to meaningfully understand, defend against, or knowingly accept the actual or potential adverse immigration consequences of a plea of guilty or nolo contendere, or (2) newly discovered evidence of actual innocence exists that requires vacation of a conviction or sentence as a matter of law or in the interests of justice. Tabs F-G.

Because relief under section 1473.7(a) of the California Penal Code is only available if based on a ground of legal invalidity, such relief completely eliminates Respondent's conviction and/or sentence and its immigration consequences. *See Matter of Pickering*, 23 I&N Dec. 621 (BIA 2003) (a conviction vacated because it is legally defective will not constitute a conviction for immigration purposes); *see also Matter of Rodriguez-Ruiz*, 22 I&N Dec. 1378 (BIA 2000) (according full faith and credit to a New York court's vacatur of a conviction on the merits); *Matter of Adamiak*, 23 I&N Dec. 878 (BIA 2006) (conviction vacated for failure to give legislatively required advisal of immigration consequences is eliminated for immigration purposes); *Nath v. Gonzales*, 467 F.3d 1185, 1187-89 (9th Cir. 2006) (conviction vacated because of a procedural or substantive defect is not considered a conviction for immigration purposes and cannot serve as the basis for removability).

Furthermore, courts have routinely reopened proceedings where a conviction that formed the basis for a removal or deportation order has been vacated due to substantive or procedural defects and have routinely overlooked the untimeliness of a motion to reopen under these circumstance. *See, e.g. Wiedersperg v. INS*, 896 F.2d 1179, 1182-83 (9th Cir. 1990) (alien was entitled to reopen proceedings where state conviction was vacated); *Cruz v. Attorney General*,

452 F.3d 240, 246 & n.3 (3d Cir. 2006) (a motion to reopen is the proper means for an alien who has been ordered removed due to a conviction to challenge his removal after that conviction is vacated) (listing cases); *Toledo-Hernandez v. Mukasey*, 521 F.3d 332, 335 n.2 (5th Cir. 2008) (same); *see also Othmane Idy*, A096-41- 986, 2012 Immig. Rptr. LEXIS 6015 (BIA, Sept. 28, 2012); *Basilio Estevez*, A044-921-877, 2012 Immig. Rptr. LEXIS 27 (BIA, Jan. 18, 2012); *Cesar Gomez-Rivas*, A041-830-317 (BIA Sept. 27, 2011); *Jacinto Moises Carbonell-Desliz*, A074-054-226, 2014 WL 347664 (BIA Jan. 13, 2014).

Therefore, because Respondent's 2004 possession conviction and his 2007 identify theft conviction have been vacated pursuant to section 1473.7 of the California Penal Code and because Respondent is no longer removable as charged, the instant proceedings should be reopened and terminated.

1. **Respondent's Motion is Timely Filed Within 90 Days of the State Court Order Vacating His 2004 and 2007 Convictions.**

In the present case, this motion is timely filed within 90 days of the state court's vacatur of Respondent's 2004 and 2007 convictions. *See, e.g., William v. Gonzales*, 499 F.3d 329, 331 (4th Cir. 2007) (treating motion to reopen filed within 90 days of vacatur as timely filed); *Pruidze v. Holder*, 632 F.3d 234, 235 (6th Cir. 2011) (same).

B. **Alternatively, This Court Should Reopen the Instant Proceedings** *Sua Sponte.*

Alternatively, Respondent moves this Court to exercise it *sua sponte* authority to reopen his removal proceedings based on extraordinary circumstances, i.e. the vacatur of his 2004 and 2007 convictions and the fact that he is no longer removable from the United States as charged. Furthermore, Respondent urges this Court to consider the fact that Respondent has been on an Order of Supervision since February 2012, that he has been reporting with ICE since that time with no issues, that ICE has not been able to remove Respondent to Iran, that he has had no legal problems since his removal order, and in general, that he has been a contributing, hardworking, member of society. Tabs D-I; *see also* 8 C.F.R. § 1003.23(b)(1) (an Immigration Judge may upon his or her own motion at any time, or upon motion of the Service or the alien, reopen or reconsider any case in which he or she has made a decision, unless jurisdiction is vested with the Board of Immigration Appeals); 8 C.F.R. § 1003.10(b) (in deciding the individual cases before them, and subject to the applicable governing standards, immigration judges shall exercise their independent judgment and discretion and may take any action consistent with their authorities under the Act and regulations that is appropriate and necessary for the disposition of such cases); *Matter of J-J-*, 21 I&N Dec. 976 (BIA 1997); *Toledo-Hernandez v. Mukasey*, 521 F.3d 332, 335 n.2 (5th Cir. 2008) (the Board has shown a willingness to *sua sponte* reopen cases where there is evidence that an immigrant's conviction was vacated for substantive or procedural defects); *Cruz v. Attorney General, supra* (the Board has routinely been willing to overlook the untimeliness of an alien's motion to reopen when a conviction supporting a removal order is vacated and urged to be invalid under *Pickering*).

IV.
CONCLUSION

For the forgoing reasons, Respondent is no longer removable as charged and therefore, this Court should reopen and terminate his removal proceedings.

Dated: February 22, 2019

Respectfully submitted,

Christopher A. Reed
Attorney at Law

EXHIBITS

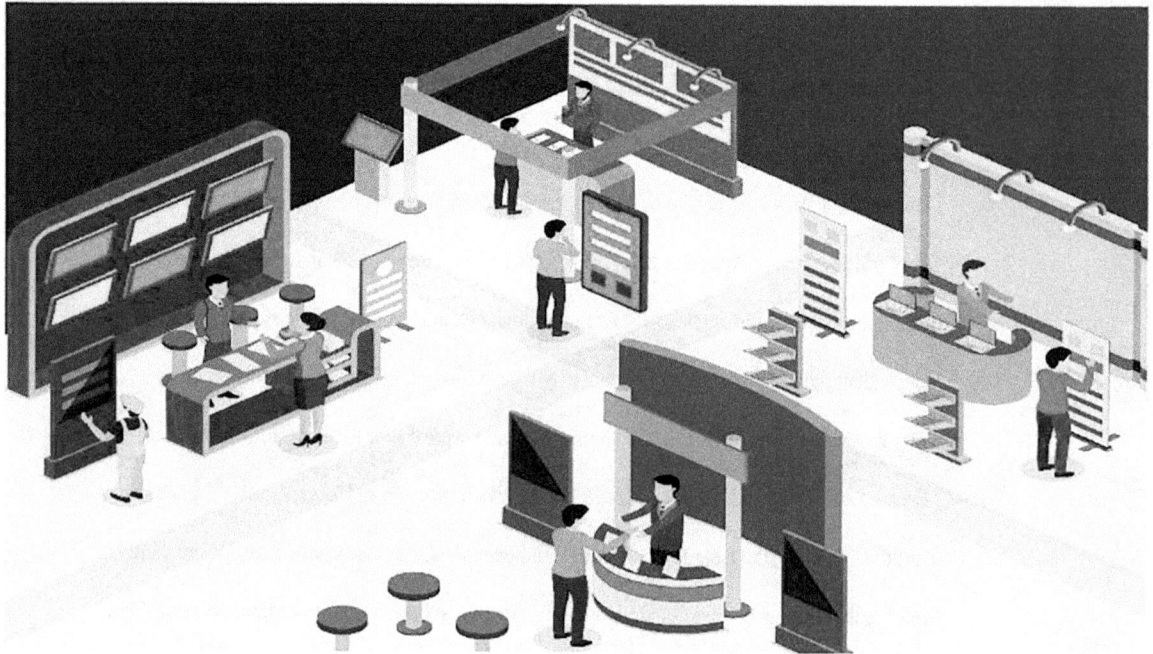

EXHIBIT '1':

Respondent's Expired Permanent Resident Card

PERMANENT RESIDENT CARD

INS A# 043-060-718
Birthdate   Category   Sex
03/21/78   P25   M
Country of Birth
Iran
CARD EXPIRES 01/02/12
Resident Since 08/29/91

C1USA0430607180WAC0129556506<<
7603215M1201022IRN<<<<<<<<<<<3
<<<<<<<<<<<<<<

U.S. DEPARTMENT OF JUSTICE Immigration and Naturalization Service

PERMANENT RESIDENT CARD

The person identified by this card is authorized to work and reside in the U.S.

EXHIBIT '2':

Respondent's Employment Authorization Card

UNITED STATES OF AMERICA
EMPLOYMENT AUTHORIZATION

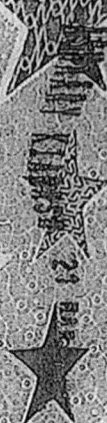

Surname

Given Name

USCIS#

Category Card#

C18   MSC

Country of Birth

Iran

Terms and Conditions

Date of Birth
21 MAR 1976 M   Sex

Valid From: 03/27/18

Card Expires   03/26/19

NOT VALID FOR REENTRY TO U.S.

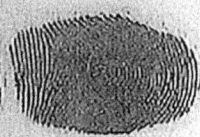

10

EXHIBIT '3':

Respondent's Partner's Naturalization Certificate

No. 25532337

INS Registration No.

Personal description of holder as of date of naturalization:

Date of birth: JANUARY 1, 1949

Sex: FEMALE

Height: 5 feet 3 inches

Marital status: DIVORCED

Country of former nationality: IRAN

I certify that the description given is true, and that the photograph affixed hereto is a likeness of me.

(Complete and true signature of holder)

Be it known that, pursuant to an application filed with the Attorney General

at: LOS ANGELES, CA

The Attorney General having found that:

then residing in the United States, intends to reside in the United States when so required by the Naturalization Laws of the United States, and had in all other respects complied with the applicable provisions of such naturalization laws and was entitled to be admitted to citizenship, such person having taken the oath of allegiance in a ceremony conducted by the

U.S. DISTRICT COURT
FOR THE CENTRAL DIST. OF CALIFORNIA

at: LOS ANGELES, CA

on: MARCH 29, 2000

that such person is admitted as a citizen of the United States of America.

Commissioner of Immigration and Naturalization

FORM N-550 REV. 6-91

EXHIBIT '4':

Letter from Respondent's Pastor

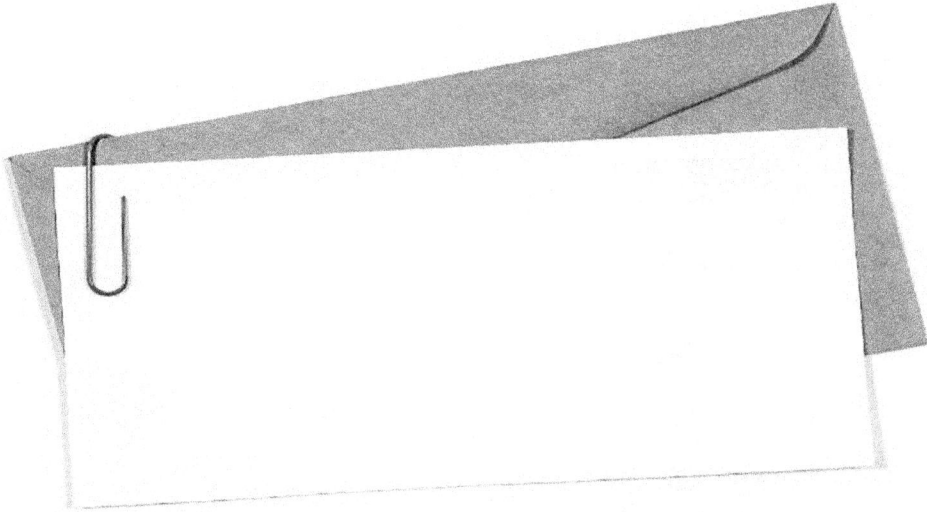

Persian Christian Church

www.persianchristianchurch.org

February 21, 2019

To whom it may concern;

My name is ███████████ and I am the lead pastor of the Persian Christian Church (PCC), which has two physical locations. We serve the San Fernando Valley community in the city of Reseda, and the Orange County Community within the city of Irvine.

PCC has been part of the Farsi speaking community of Southern California since 1989 and it continues to be a beacon of light for those who seek the Truth.

Over two years ago ████████████████ contacted me over the phone and we spoke about his interest to attend one of our evening services at the Irvine Persian Christian Church (iPCC). A week or so later Kiarash attended our mid-week, Thursday night, Bible study gathering and that is when and where we met face to face for the very first time.

Since then ██████ has committed to the Persian Christian Church in Irvine whole heartedly. In the beginning he was attending all Sunday evening and Thursday evening services as someone who was simply interested, but after a very short time he committed himself to the church and has been an active member of the church.

██████, not only began to actively attend church and grow spiritually but also was recommended by our deacons, to join few of the church ministries. Currently ██████ is part of the ushering team, which is responsible for all aspects of the operation of the Sunday evening service. He usually works within a team of three additional individuals and their team coordinates closely with our Sunday school, hospitality and media team. ████████ has also been in charge of few of our special events, such as Christmas celebration along with our annual seminars. Furthermore last November and December ████████ was the point of contact between iPCC and the Orange County Rescue Mission, which is a nonprofit organization providing food and shelter for the homeless population of greater OC area. Through this venture and by the direct leadership and coordination of ████████ iPCC was able to provide over 500 hot meals and over $1500 in gift for the children and their parents, staying at the Orange County Rescue Mission. As part of Kiarash's current responsibility, he is facilitating all aspects of a trip of over 50 individuals to Israel, towards the end of the year.

These delicate and spiritual ministries in church are only given and trusted to church members, who are able to manage, direct and work well with other teams and individuals. With every single ministry opportunity given to Kiarash, he has managed to go above and beyond the ministry standard to make sure that all aspects of the event or services are well maintained and efficiently executed by him and the team that he leads. More importantly his level of proficiency and professionalism in dealing with others has been noteworthy and highly praised by the senior church staff and other members. His level of respect and consideration to and for others has been unparalleled to anything and anyone that I have personally worked with in the past 20 years.

PCC Valley 19620 Vanowen St. Reseda CA 91355 818.771.9191 mail@pccvalley.org
PCC Irvine 6000 Irvine Center Drive, Irvine, CA 92618 949.831.1020 mail@pccirvine.org

18 | P a g e

Persian
Christian
Church

www.persianchristianchurch.org

Currently Mr. ███████ is being mentored by two seasoned individuals from church, to take on the weekly financial reporting of P&L (Profits and Loss) of every Sunday service.

It is noteworthy to mention that in October of 2017, I had the privilege and honor of baptizing ███ in water, which is one of the two Holy Sacraments of the Assemblies of God Church.

███████ contribution to his church family is just a very small example of his attitude and perspective towards his own life and the people around him. He is a stellar individual that not only is a joy to be around but also brings the best out of those around him.

Individuals like ███████ are people that our society not only needs but can take examples from. I have proudly and repeatedly used his humble spirit and his tender heart in my sermons to show how God is able to use an individual to impact a church and those within it.

Numerous times ████ and I have had some one on one and heart to heart conversations. He has been very open and upfront with me in regards to his past, his mistakes and the darker times of his adult life. What I have always taken from our conversations has been the fact that he has taken full responsibility for what he has done and what he went through and has never shifted the blame to a particular event or individual. As his pastor, I truly admire his recognition of mistakes made and applaud his decisions to turn his life around. Kiarash is a walking example of what determination can mean and what it looks like in a society if an individual is given a new chance.

At our church ████ is the very definition of trust, respect and a true friend in times of need. Needless to say but must be mentioned is his interaction with his family, specifically his dear mother. I have yet to meet someone who is as caring, loving and generous than Kiarash towards anyone.

Many times I have mentioned to ██████ that he is an answer to many of my personal prayers. Our church, our city and our society needs more people like ████ He is someone who has seen the worst and is now living the best and yet striving towards excellence. I am honored to have come to know him, to be able to mentor him spiritually and to call him a true friend.

It is an honor to be able to serve God and His people with ███████ Should you have any further questions, please feel free to contact me.

Rev. Jonathan J. Nazanin

Lead Pastor

PCC Valley 19620 Vanowen St. Reseda, CA 91335 818.771.9191 mail@pccvalley.org
PCC Irvine 6000 Irvine Center Drive, Irvine, CA 92618 949.831.1020 mail@pccirvine.org

19 | P a g e

EXHIBIT '5':

Respondent's 2017 Income Tax Return and 1099

PAYER'S name, street address, city or town, state or province, country, ZIP or foreign postal code, and telephone no.

	OMB No. 1545-0115	Miscellaneous Income
1 Rents $	**2017**	
2 Royalties $	Form 1099-MISC	
3 Other income $	4 Federal income tax withheld $	**Copy B For Recipient**
5 Fishing boat proceeds $	6 Medical and health care payments $	

PAYER'S federal identification number

77-0609275

RECIPIENT'S identification number

7 Nonemployee compensation $ **46140.52**	8 Substitute payments in lieu of dividends or interest $	This is important tax information and is being furnished to the Internal Revenue Service. If you are required to file a return, a negligence penalty or other sanction may be imposed on you if this income is taxable and the IRS determines that it has not been reported.
9 Payer made direct sales of $5,000 or more of consumer products to a buyer (recipient) for resale ▶ ☐	10 Crop insurance proceeds $	
11	12	

RECIPIENT'S name, street address (including apt. no.) city or town, state or province, country, and ZIP or foreign postal code

Mission Viejo CA 92691

13 Excess golden parachute payments $	14 Gross proceeds paid to an attorney $	

Account number (see instructions)

FATCA filing requirement ☐

16 State tax withheld $ _____ $ _____	17 State/Payer's state no.	18 State income $ _____ $ _____

15a Section 409A deferrals $	15b Section 409A income $	

Form **1099-MISC**   (keep for your records)   www.irs.gov/form1099misc   Department of the Treasury - Internal Revenue Service

Form 1040   Department of the Treasury—Internal Revenue Service   (99)

U.S. Individual Income Tax Return   **2017**   OMB No. 1545-0074   IRS Use Only—Do not write or staple in this space.

For the year Jan. 1–Dec. 31, 2017, or other tax year beginning _____, 2017, ending _____, 20____   See separate instructions.

Your first name and initial	Last name	Your social security number
▮▮▮	▮▮▮	▮▮▮
If a joint return, spouse's first name and initial	Last name	Spouse's social security number

Home address (number and street). If you have a P.O. box, see instructions.   Apt. no. ▮▮▮

▲ Make sure the SSN(s) above and on line 6c are correct.

City, town or post office, state, and ZIP code. If you have a foreign address, also complete spaces below (see instructions). ▮▮▮

Presidential Election Campaign
Check here if you, or your spouse if filing jointly, want $3 to go to this fund. Checking a box below will not change your tax or refund. ☐ You ☐ Spouse

Foreign country name ▮▮▮   Foreign province/state/county   Foreign postal code

Filing Status
Check only one box.

1. ☒ Single
2. ☐ Married filing jointly (even if only one had income)
3. ☐ Married filing separately. Enter spouse's SSN above and full name here. ▶
4. ☐ Head of household (with qualifying person). (See instructions.) If the qualifying person is a child but not your dependent, enter this child's name here. ▶
5. ☐ Qualifying widow(er) (see instructions)

Exemptions

6a ☒ Yourself. If someone can claim you as a dependent, do not check box 6a . . . . .
b ☐ Spouse . . . .

c Dependents:

(1) First name Last name	(2) Dependent's social security number	(3) Dependent's relationship to you	(4) ✓ if child under age 17 qualifying for child tax credit (see instructions)
▮▮▮	▮▮▮	Parent	☐
			☐
			☐
			☐

If more than four dependents, see instructions and check here ▶ ☐

Boxes checked on 6a and 6b — **1**

No. of children on 6c who:
• lived with you
• did not live with you due to divorce or separation (see instructions)

Dependents on 6c not entered above — **1**

Add numbers on lines above ▶ **2**

d Total number of exemptions claimed . . . .

Income

Attach Form(s) W-2 here. Also attach Forms W-2G and 1099-R if tax was withheld.

If you did not get a W-2, see instructions.

7	Wages, salaries, tips, etc. Attach Form(s) W-2	7	918.
8a	Taxable interest. Attach Schedule B if required	8a	
b	Tax-exempt interest. Do not include on line 8a . . . 8b		
9a	Ordinary dividends. Attach Schedule B if required	9a	
b	Qualified dividends 9b		
10	Taxable refunds, credits, or offsets of state and local income taxes . .	10	
11	Alimony received	11	
12	Business income or (loss). Attach Schedule C or C-EZ	12	24,619.
13	Capital gain or (loss). Attach Schedule D if required. If not required, check here ▶ ☐	13	
14	Other gains or (losses). Attach Form 4797	14	
15a	IRA distributions . 15a _____ b Taxable amount . . .	15b	
16a	Pensions and annuities 16a _____ b Taxable amount . . .	16b	
17	Rental real estate, royalties, partnerships, S corporations, trusts, etc. Attach Schedule E	17	
18	Farm income or (loss). Attach Schedule F	18	
19	Unemployment compensation	19	
20a	Social security benefits 20a _____ b Taxable amount . . .	20b	
21	Other income. List type and amount _____	21	
22	Combine the amounts in the far right column for lines 7 through 21. This is your total income ▶	22	25,537.

Adjusted Gross Income

23	Educator expenses 23		
24	Certain business expenses of reservists, performing artists, and fee-basis government officials. Attach Form 2106 or 2106-EZ 24		
25	Health savings account deduction. Attach Form 8889 . 25		
26	Moving expenses. Attach Form 3903 . . . 26		
27	Deductible part of self-employment tax. Attach Schedule SE . 27 1,740.		
28	Self-employed SEP, SIMPLE, and qualified plans . 28		
29	Self-employed health insurance deduction 29		
30	Penalty on early withdrawal of savings 30		
31a	Alimony paid b Recipient's SSN ▶ _____ 31a		
32	IRA deduction 32		
33	Student loan interest deduction 33		
34	Tuition and fees. Attach Form 8917 34		
35	Domestic production activities deduction. Attach Form 8903 35		
36	Add lines 23 through 35	36	1,740.
37	Subtract line 36 from line 22. This is your adjusted gross income . . . . ▶	37	23,797.

For Disclosure, Privacy Act, and Paperwork Reduction Act Notice, see separate instructions.   BAA   REV 02/22/18 PRO   Form **1040** (2017)

Tax and Credits	38	Amount from line 37 (adjusted gross income)		38	23,797.
	39a	Check { You were born before January 2, 1953, ☐ Blind.　☐ Spouse was born before January 2, 1953, ☐ Blind. } Total boxes checked ▶ 39a			
	b	If your spouse itemizes on a separate return or you were a dual-status alien, check here▶ 39b☐			
Standard Deduction for—	40	Itemized deductions (from Schedule A) or your standard deduction (see left margin)		40	19,290.
• People who check any box on line 39a or 39b or who can be claimed as a dependent, see instructions.	41	Subtract line 40 from line 38		41	4,507.
	42	Exemptions. If line 38 is $156,900 or less, multiply $4,050 by the number on line 6d. Otherwise, see instructions		42	8,100.
	43	Taxable income. Subtract line 42 from line 41. If line 42 is more than line 41, enter -0-		43	0.
	44	Tax (see instructions). Check if any from: a ☐ Form(s) 8814　b ☐ Form 4972　c ☐		44	0.
• All others:	45	Alternative minimum tax (see instructions). Attach Form 6251		45	
Single or Married filing separately, $6,350	46	Excess advance premium tax credit repayment. Attach Form 8962		46	
	47	Add lines 44, 45, and 46	▶	47	0.
Married filing jointly or Qualifying widow(er), $12,700	48	Foreign tax credit. Attach Form 1116 if required	48		
	49	Credit for child and dependent care expenses. Attach Form 2441	49		
	50	Education credits from Form 8863, line 19	50		
	51	Retirement savings contributions credit. Attach Form 8880	51		
Head of household, $9,350	52	Child tax credit. Attach Schedule 8812, if required	52		
	53	Residential energy credits. Attach Form 5695	53		
	54	Other credits from Form: a ☐ 3800 b ☐ 8801 c ☐	54		
	55	Add lines 48 through 54. These are your total credits		55	
	56	Subtract line 55 from line 47. If line 55 is more than line 47, enter -0-	▶	56	0.
Other Taxes	57	Self-employment tax. Attach Schedule SE		57	3,479.
	58	Unreported social security and Medicare tax from Form: a ☐ 4137 b ☐ 8919		58	
	59	Additional tax on IRAs, other qualified retirement plans, etc. Attach Form 5329 if required		59	
	60a	Household employment taxes from Schedule H		60a	
	b	First-time homebuyer credit repayment. Attach Form 5405 if required		60b	
	61	Health care: individual responsibility (see instructions)　Full-year coverage ☒		61	
	62	Taxes from: a ☐ Form 8959 b ☐ Form 8960 c ☐ Instructions; enter code(s)		62	
	63	Add lines 56 through 62. This is your total tax	▶	63	3,479.
Payments	64	Federal income tax withheld from Forms W-2 and 1099	64		
If you have a qualifying child, attach Schedule EIC.	65	2017 estimated tax payments and amount applied from 2016 return	65		
	66a	Earned income credit (EIC)　.　No	66a		
	b	Nontaxable combat pay election	66b		
	67	Additional child tax credit. Attach Schedule 8812	67		
	68	American opportunity credit from Form 8863, line 8	68		
	69	Net premium tax credit. Attach Form 8962	69	702.	
	70	Amount paid with request for extension to file	70		
	71	Excess social security and tier 1 RRTA tax withheld	71		
	72	Credit for federal tax on fuels. Attach Form 4136	72		
	73	Credits from Form: a ☐ 2439 b ☐ Reserved c ☐ 8885 d ☐	73		
	74	Add lines 64, 65, 66a, and 67 through 73. These are your total payments	▶	74	702.
Refund	75	If line 74 is more than line 63, subtract line 63 from line 74. This is the amount you overpaid		75	
	76a	Amount of line 75 you want refunded to you. If Form 8888 is attached, check here ▶ ☐		76a	
Direct deposit? See Instructions.	b	Routing number X X X X X X X X X ▶ Type: ☐ Checking ☐ Savings			
	d	Account number X X X X X X X X X X X X X X X X X			
	77	Amount of line 75 you want applied to your 2018 estimated tax ▶ 77			
Amount You Owe	78	Amount you owe. Subtract line 74 from line 63. For details on how to pay, see instructions ▶		78	2,843.
	79	Estimated tax penalty (see instructions)	79	66.	

Sign Here Joint return? See instructions. Keep a copy for your records.	Under penalties of perjury, I declare that I have examined this return and accompanying schedules and statements, and to the best of my knowledge and belief, they are true, correct, and accurately list all amounts and sources of income I received during the tax year. Declaration of preparer (other than taxpayer) is based on all information of which preparer has any knowledge.
	Your signature　　Date　　Your occupation S/E　　Daytime phone number (949) 716-7949
	Spouse's signature. If a joint return, both must sign.　Date　Spouse's occupation　　If the IRS sent you an Identity Protection PIN, enter it here (see inst.)

Paid Preparer Use Only	Print/Type preparer's name REZA AZADI	Preparer's signature	Date	Check ☐ if self-employed	PTIN P01513002
	Firm's name ▶ Professional Financial Services			Firm's EIN ▶ 33-0891189	
	Firm's address ▶ 151 Kalmus Dr Ste C210 Costa Mesa CA 92626			Phone no.	

Go to www.irs.gov/Form1040 for instructions and the latest information.　　　　REV 02/22/18 PRO　Form **1040** (2017)

SCHEDULE A
(Form 1040)

Department of the Treasury
Internal Revenue Service (99)

Name(s) shown on Form 1040

Itemized Deductions

▶ Go to www.irs.gov/ScheduleA for instructions and the latest information.
▶ Attach to Form 1040.
Caution: If you are claiming a net qualified disaster loss on Form 4684, see the instructions for line 28.

OMB No. 1545-0074

2017

Attachment
Sequence No. **07**

Your social security number

Medical and Dental Expenses		Caution: Do not include expenses reimbursed or paid by others.		
	1	Medical and dental expenses (see instructions)	1	1,686.
	2	Enter amount from Form 1040, line 38 2 23,797.		
	3	Multiply line 2 by 7.5% (0.075).	3	1,785.
	4	Subtract line 3 from line 1. If line 3 is more than line 1, enter -0-	4	0.
Taxes You Paid	5	State and local (check only one box):		
		a ☐ Income taxes, or	5	586.
		b ☒ General sales taxes		
	6	Real estate taxes (see instructions)	6	5,884.
	7	Personal property taxes	7	327.
	8	Other taxes. List type and amount ▶ _____	8	
	9	Add lines 5 through 8	9	6,797.
Interest You Paid	10	Home mortgage interest and points reported to you on Form 1098	10	10,373.
	11	Home mortgage interest not reported to you on Form 1098. If paid to the person from whom you bought the home, see instructions and show that person's name, identifying no., and address ▶		
Note: Your mortgage interest deduction may be limited (see instructions).		_____ _____	11	
	12	Points not reported to you on Form 1098. See instructions for special rules	12	
	13	Mortgage insurance premiums (see instructions)	13	
	14	Investment interest. Attach Form 4952 if required. See instructions	14	
	15	Add lines 10 through 14	15	10,373.
Gifts to Charity	16	Gifts by cash or check. If you made any gift of $250 or more, see instructions.	16	1,870.
If you made a gift and got a benefit for it, see instructions.	17	Other than by cash or check. If any gift of $250 or more, see instructions. You must attach Form 8283 if over $500 . . .	17	250.
	18	Carryover from prior year	18	
	19	Add lines 16 through 18	19	2,120.
Casualty and Theft Losses	20	Casualty or theft loss(es) other than net qualified disaster losses. Attach Form 4684 and enter the amount from line 16 of that form. See instructions	20	
Job Expenses and Certain Miscellaneous Deductions	21	Unreimbursed employee expenses—job travel, union dues, job education, etc. Attach Form 2106 or 2106-EZ if required. See instructions. ▶ _____	21	
	22	Tax preparation fees	22	
	23	Other expenses—investment, safe deposit box, etc. List type and amount ▶ _____	23	
	24	Add lines 21 through 23	24	
	25	Enter amount from Form 1040, line 38 25		
	26	Multiply line 25 by 2% (0.02)	26	
	27	Subtract line 26 from line 24. If line 26 is more than line 24, enter -0-	27	
Other Miscellaneous Deductions	28	Other—from list in instructions. List type and amount ▶ _____	28	
Total Itemized Deductions	29	Is Form 1040, line 38, over $156,900?		
		☒ No. Your deduction is not limited. Add the amounts in the far right column for lines 4 through 28. Also, enter this amount on Form 1040, line 40.	29	19,290.
		☐ Yes. Your deduction may be limited. See the Itemized Deductions Worksheet in the instructions to figure the amount to enter.		
	30	If you elect to itemize deductions even though they are less than your standard deduction, check here . . . . ▶ ☐		

For Paperwork Reduction Act Notice, see the Instructions for Form 1040.   BAA   REV 02/22/18 PRO   Schedule A (Form 1040) 2017

Profit or Loss From Business
(Sole Proprietorship)

▶ Go to www.irs.gov/ScheduleC for instructions and the latest information.
▶ Attach to Form 1040, 1040NR, or 1041; partnerships generally must file Form 1065.

OMB No. 1545-0074

2017

Attachment
Sequence No. 09

Name of proprietor	Social security number (SSN)
	607-44-7640

A	Principal business or profession, including product or service (see instructions)	B Enter code from instructions
	NETWORKING	▶

C	Business name. If no separate business name, leave blank.	D Employer ID number (EIN) (see instr.)
	3 S. NETWORK, INC.	

E	Business address (including suite or room no.) ▶
	City, town or post office, state, and ZIP code

F	Accounting method:	(1) ☒ Cash	(2) ☐ Accrual	(3) ☐ Other (specify) ▶		
G	Did you "materially participate" in the operation of this business during 2017? If "No," see instructions for limit on losses				☒ Yes	☐ No
H	If you started or acquired this business during 2017, check here				▶ ☐	
I	Did you make any payments in 2017 that would require you to file Form(s) 1099? (see instructions)				☒ Yes	☐ No
J	If "Yes," did you or will you file required Forms 1099?				☒ Yes	☐ No

Part I Income

1	Gross receipts or sales. See instructions for line 1 and check the box if this income was reported to you on Form W-2 and the "Statutory employee" box on that form was checked . . . . ▶ ☐	1	46,141.
2	Returns and allowances . .	2	
3	Subtract line 2 from line 1	3	46,141.
4	Cost of goods sold (from line 42)	4	
5	Gross profit. Subtract line 4 from line 3	5	46,141.
6	Other income, including federal and state gasoline or fuel tax credit or refund (see instructions) . . .	6	
7	Gross income. Add lines 5 and 6 . . . . ▶	7	46,141.

Part II Expenses. Enter expenses for business use of your home only on line 30.

8	Advertising	8	705.	18	Office expense (see instructions)	18	1,527.
9	Car and truck expenses (see instructions)	9	5,688.	19	Pension and profit-sharing plans .	19	
				20	Rent or lease (see instructions):		
10	Commissions and fees .	10		a	Vehicles, machinery, and equipment	20a	
11	Contract labor (see instructions)	11		b	Other business property . . .	20b	
12	Depletion	12		21	Repairs and maintenance . . .	21	2,954.
13	Depreciation and section 179 expense deduction (not included in Part II) (see instructions). . . .	13	381.	22	Supplies (not included in Part II) .	22	2,661.
				23	Taxes and licenses	23	645.
				24	Travel, meals, and entertainment:		
14	Employee benefit programs (other than on line 19) . .	14		a	Travel	24a	
15	Insurance (other than health)	15	2,400.	b	Deductible meals and entertainment (see instructions)	24b	578.
16	Interest:			25	Utilities	25	
a	Mortgage (paid to banks, etc.)	16a		26	Wages (less employment credits).	26	
b	Other	16b		27a	Other expenses (from line 48) . .	27a	3,533.
17	Legal and professional services	17	450.	b	Reserved for future use . . .	27b	
28	Total expenses before expenses for business use of home. Add lines 8 through 27a . . . . . ▶					28	21,522.
29	Tentative profit or (loss). Subtract line 28 from line 7					29	24,619.
30	Expenses for business use of your home. Do not report these expenses elsewhere. Attach Form 8829 unless using the simplified method (see instructions). Simplified method filers only: enter the total square footage of: (a) your home: _____ and (b) the part of your home used for business: _____. Use the Simplified Method Worksheet in the instructions to figure the amount to enter on line 30					30	
31	Net profit or (loss). Subtract line 30 from line 29. • If a profit, enter on both Form 1040, line 12 (or Form 1040NR, line 13) and on Schedule SE, line 2. (If you checked the box on line 1, see instructions). Estates and trusts, enter on Form 1041, line 3. • If a loss, you must go to line 32.					31	24,619.
32	If you have a loss, check the box that describes your investment in this activity (see instructions). • If you checked 32a, enter the loss on both Form 1040, line 12, (or Form 1040NR, line 13) and on Schedule SE, line 2. (If you checked the box on line 1, see the line 31 instructions). Estates and trusts, enter on Form 1041, line 3. • If you checked 32b, you must attach Form 6198. Your loss may be limited.				32a ☐ All investment is at risk. 32b ☐ Some investment is not at risk.		

For Paperwork Reduction Act Notice, see the separate instructions. BAA   REV 11/15/17 PRO   Schedule C (Form 1040) 2017

SCHEDULE SE (Form 1040)	Self-Employment Tax	OMB No. 1545-0074
Department of the Treasury Internal Revenue Service (99)	▶ Go to www.irs.gov/ScheduleSE for instructions and the latest information. ▶ Attach to Form 1040 or Form 1040NR.	2017 Attachment Sequence No. 17

Name of person with self-employment income (as shown on Form 1040 or Form 1040NR)	Social security number of person with self-employment income ▶
▓▓▓▓▓	▓▓▓▓▓

Before you begin: To determine if you must file Schedule SE, see the instructions.

May I Use Short Schedule SE or Must I Use Long Schedule SE?

Note: Use this flowchart only if you must file Schedule SE. If unsure, see *Who Must File Schedule SE* in the instructions.

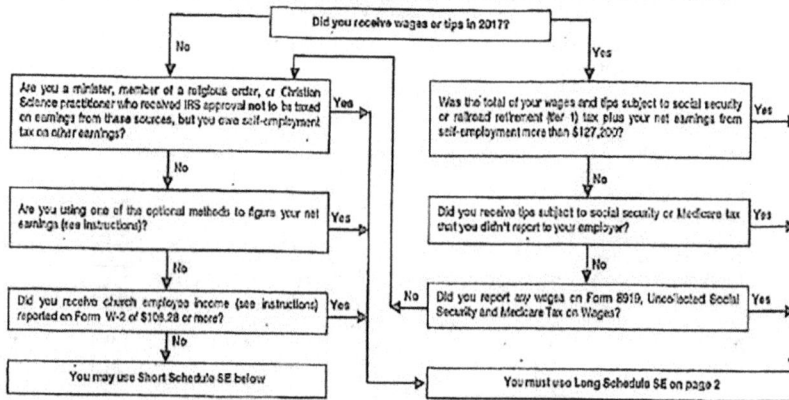

Did you receive wages or tips in 2017?

- No → Are you a minister, member of a religious order, or Christian Science practitioner who received IRS approval **not** to be taxed on earnings from these sources, but you owe self-employment tax on *other* earnings?
  - Yes →
  - No → Are you using one of the optional methods to figure your net earnings (see instructions)?
    - Yes →
    - No → Did you receive church employee income (see instructions) reported on Form W-2 of $108.28 or more?
      - Yes →
      - No → **You may use Short Schedule SE below**
- Yes → Was the total of your wages and tips subject to social security or railroad retirement (tier 1) tax plus your net earnings from self-employment more than $127,200?
  - Yes →
  - No → Did you receive tips subject to social security or Medicare tax that you didn't report to your employer?
    - Yes →
    - No → Did you report any wages on Form 8919, Uncollected Social Security and Medicare Tax on Wages?
      - No →
      - Yes → **You must use Long Schedule SE on page 2**

Section A—Short Schedule SE. Caution: Read above to see if you can use Short Schedule SE.

1a	Net farm profit or (loss) from Schedule F, line 34, and farm partnerships, Schedule K-1 (Form 1065), box 14, code A	1a	
b	If you received social security retirement or disability benefits, enter the amount of Conservation Reserve Program payments included on Schedule F, line 4b, or listed on Schedule K-1 (Form 1065), box 20, code Z	1b (	)
2	Net profit or (loss) from Schedule C, line 31; Schedule C-EZ, line 3; Schedule K-1 (Form 1065), box 14, code A (other than farming); and Schedule K-1 (Form 1065-B), box 9, code J1. Ministers and members of religious orders, see instructions for types of income to report on this line. See instructions for other income to report	2	24,619.
3	Combine lines 1a, 1b, and 2	3	24,619.
4	Multiply line 3 by 92.35% (0.9235). If less than $400, you don't owe self-employment tax; don't file this schedule unless you have an amount on line 1b . . . . ▶	4	22,736.
	Note: If line 4 is less than $400 due to Conservation Reserve Program payments on line 1b, see instructions.		
5	Self-employment tax. If the amount on line 4 is:		
	• $127,200 or less, multiply line 4 by 15.3% (0.153). Enter the result here and on Form 1040, line 57, or Form 1040NR, line 55		
	• More than $127,200, multiply line 4 by 2.9% (0.029). Then, add $15,772.80 to the result. Enter the total here and on Form 1040, line 57, or Form 1040NR, line 55	5	3,479.
6	Deduction for one-half of self-employment tax. Multiply line 5 by 50% (0.50). Enter the result here and on Form 1040, line 27, or Form 1040NR, line 27	6	1,740.

For Paperwork Reduction Act Notice, see your tax return instructions. BAA   REV 11/14/17 PRO   Schedule SE (Form 1040) 2017

Part III Cost of Goods Sold (see instructions)

33 Method(s) used to value closing inventory: a ☐ Cost b ☐ Lower of cost or market c ☐ Other (attach explanation)

34 Was there any change in determining quantities, costs, or valuations between opening and closing inventory?
If "Yes," attach explanation . . . .   ☐ Yes   ☐ No

35	Inventory at beginning of year. If different from last year's closing inventory, attach explanation . . .	35	
36	Purchases less cost of items withdrawn for personal use	36	
37	Cost of labor. Do not include any amounts paid to yourself	37	
38	Materials and supplies	38	
39	Other costs.	39	
40	Add lines 35 through 39	40	
41	Inventory at end of year	41	
42	Cost of goods sold. Subtract line 41 from line 40. Enter the result here and on line 4	42	

Part IV Information on Your Vehicle. Complete this part only if you are claiming car or truck expenses on line 9 and are not required to file Form 4562 for this business. See the instructions for line 13 to find out if you must file Form 4562.

43 When did you place your vehicle in service for business purposes? (month, day, year) ▶ 02/15/2017

44 Of the total number of miles you drove your vehicle during 2017, enter the number of miles you used your vehicle for:

a Business __7,500__ b Commuting (see instructions) __2,000__ c Other __3,500__

45 Was your vehicle available for personal use during off-duty hours? . . . . ☒ Yes ☐ No

46 Do you (or your spouse) have another vehicle available for personal use?. . . . . ☐ Yes ☒ No

47a Do you have evidence to support your deduction? . . . . ☐ Yes ☒ No

b If "Yes," is the evidence written? . . . . ☐ Yes ☐ No

Part V Other Expenses. List below business expenses not included on lines 8–26 or line 30.

TELPHONE & CELL	1,583.
SUIT & ASS.	1,950.
48 Total other expenses. Enter here and on line 27a 48	3,533.

TAXABLE YEAR

2017 **California Resident Income Tax Return**

FORM

540

APE

ATTACH FEDERAL RETURN

17   PBA   519100

A
f:
RF

███████████████

███████████████

03-21-1976

1 [X] Single		**4** [ ] Head of household (with qualifying person). See instructions.	
2 [ ] Married/RDP filing jointly. See inst.		**5** [ ] Qualifying widow(er) with dependent child. Enter year spouse/RDP died	
3 [ ] Married/RDP filing separately. Enter spouse's/RDP's SSN or ITIN above and full name here			

If your California filing status is different from your federal filing status, check the box here .... [ ]

6 If someone can claim you (or your spouse/RDP) as a dependent, check the box here. See inst....... ⊙ **6** [ ]

▶ For line 7, line 8, line 9, and line 10: Multiply the amount you enter in the box by the pre-printed dollar amount for that line.   Whole dollars only

7 Personal: If you checked box 1, 3, or 4 above, enter 1 in the box. If you checked box 2 or 5, enter 2, in the box. If you checked the box on line 6, see instructions.. ⊙ **7** [1] X $114 = ⊙ $ | 114

8 Blind: If you (or your spouse/RDP) are visually impaired, enter 1; If both are visually impaired, enter 2 .... ⊙ **8** [ ] X $114 = ⊙ $ |

9 Senior: If you (or your spouse/RDP) are 65 or older, enter 1; If both are 65 or older, enter 2 .... ⊙ **9** [ ] X $114 = ⊙ $ |

10 Dependents: Do not include yourself or your spouse/RDP.

	Dependent 1	Dependent 2	Dependent 3
First Name	⊙ ████	⊙	⊙
Last Name	⊙ ████	⊙	⊙
SSN	⊙ ████	⊙	⊙
Dependent's relationship to you	⊙ PARENT	⊙	⊙

Total dependent exemptions .... ⊙ **10** [1] X $353 = ⊙ $ | 353

11 Exemption amount: Add line 7 through line 10. Transfer this amount to line 32.............. ⊙ **11** $ | 467

REV 01/04/18 PRO

175   3101174

Form 540 2017   Side 1

	12	State wages from your Form(s) W-2, box 16 .... ⊙ 12	918 . 00
	13	Enter federal adjusted gross income from Form 1040, line 37; 1040A, line 21; or 1040EZ, line 4 ...... ⊙ 13	23797 . 00
	14	California adjustments – subtractions. Enter the amount from Schedule CA (540), line 37, column B .... ⊙ 14	381 . 00
	15	Subtract line 14 from line 13. If less than zero, enter the result in parentheses. See instructions 15	23416 . 00
	16	California adjustments – additions. Enter the amount from Schedule CA (540), line 37, column C .... ⊙ 16	. 00
	17	California adjusted gross income. Combine line 15 and line 16 .... ⊙ 17	23416 . 00

Taxable Income

18 Enter the larger of {
Your California itemized deductions from Schedule CA (540), line 44; OR
Your California standard deduction shown below for your filing status:
• Single or Married/RDP filing separately $4,236
• Married/RDP filing jointly, Head of household, or Qualifying widow(er) $8,472
If Married/RDP filing separately or the box on line 6 is checked, STOP. See Instructions .. } ⊙ 18 `18704 . 00`

19 Subtract line 18 from line 17. This is your taxable income. If less than zero, enter -0- .... ⊙ 19 `4712 . 00`

Tax

31	Tax. Check the box if from: [X] Tax Table [ ] Tax Rate Schedule		
	⊙ [ ] FTB 3800 ⊙ [ ] FTB 3803 .... ⊙ 31		47 . 00
32	Exemption credits. Enter the amount from line 11. If your federal AGI is more than $187,203, see instructions .... ⊙ 32		467 . 00
33	Subtract line 32 from line 31. If less than zero, enter -0- .... ⊙ 33		0 . 00
34	Tax. See instructions. Check the box if from: ⊙ [ ] Schedule G-1 ⊙ [ ] FTB 5870A .... ⊙ 34		. 00
35	Add line 33 and line 34 .... ⊙ 35		0 . 00

Special Credits

40	Nonrefundable Child and Dependent Care Expenses Credit. See instructions .... ⊙ 40	. 00
43	Enter credit name _____ code ⊙ ____ and amount .... ⊙ 43	. 00
44	Enter credit name _____ code ⊙ ____ and amount .... ⊙ 44	. 00
45	To claim more than two credits, see instructions. Attach Schedule P (540) .... ⊙ 45	. 00
46	Nonrefundable renter's credit. See instructions .... ⊙ 46	. 00
47	Add line 40 through line 46. These are your total credits .... ⊙ 47	. 00
48	Subtract line 47 from line 35. If less than zero, enter -0- .... ⊙ 48	0 . 00

Other Taxes

61	Alternative minimum tax. Attach Schedule P (540) .... ⊙ 61	. 00
62	Mental Health Services Tax. See Instructions .... ⊙ 62	. 00
63	Other taxes and credit recapture. See instructions .... ⊙ 63	. 00
64	Add line 48, line 61, line 62, and line 63. This is your total tax .... ⊙ 64	0 . 00

Your name: ███████████ Your SSN or ITIN: ███████████

Payments	71	California income tax withheld. See instructions	⊚ 71		00
	72	2017 CA estimated tax and other payments. See instructions	⊚ 72		00
	73	Withholding (Form 592-B and/or 593). See instructions	⊚ 73		00
	74	Excess SDI (or VPDI) withheld. See instructions....................................	⊚ 74		00
	75	Earned Income Tax Credit (EITC)	⊚ 75		00
	76	Add lines 71 through 75. These are your total payments. See instructions	⊚ 76		00

Use Tax	91	Use Tax. Do not leave blank. See instructions.......................	⊚ 91	0	00

If line 91 is zero, check if: [X] No use tax is owed.

[ ] You paid your use tax obligation directly to CDTFA.

Overpaid Tax/Tax Due	92	Payments balance. If line 76 is more than line 91, subtract line 91 from line 76	⊚ 92		00
	93	Use Tax balance. If line 91 is more than line 76, subtract line 76 from line 91	⊚ 93	0	00
	94	Overpaid tax. If line 92 is more than line 64, subtract line 64 from line 92	⊚ 94		00
	95	Amount of line 94 you want applied to your 2018 estimated tax	⊚ 95		00
	96	Overpaid tax available this year. Subtract line 95 from line 94	⊚ 96		00
	97	Tax due. If line 92 is less than line 64, subtract line 92 from line 64	⊚ 97	0	00

REV 01/00/18 PRO   175   3103174   Form 540 2017 Side 3

30 | P a g e

Your name: ▓▓▓▓▓▓▓▓▓▓▓▓   Your SSN or ITIN: ▓▓▓▓▓▓▓▓▓

	Code	Amount
California Seniors Special Fund. See Instructions	⊙ 400		.00
Alzheimer's Disease/Related Disorders Fund	⊙ 401		.00
Rare and Endangered Species Preservation Voluntary Tax Contribution Program	⊙ 403		.00
California Breast Cancer Research Voluntary Tax Contribution Fund	⊙ 405		.00
California Firefighters' Memorial Fund	⊙ 406		.00
Emergency Food for Families Voluntary Tax Contribution Fund	⊙ 407		.00
California Peace Officer Memorial Foundation Fund	⊙ 408		.00
California Sea Otter Fund	⊙ 410		.00
California Cancer Research Voluntary Tax Contribution Fund	⊙ 413		.00
School Supplies for Homeless Children Fund	⊙ 422		.00
State Parks Protection Fund/Parks Pass Purchase	⊙ 423		.00
Protect Our Coast and Oceans Voluntary Tax Contribution Fund	⊙ 424		.00
Keep Arts in Schools Voluntary Tax Contribution Fund	⊙ 425		.00
State Children's Trust Fund for the Prevention of Child Abuse	⊙ 430		.00
Prevention of Animal Homelessness and Cruelty Fund	⊙ 431		.00
Revive the Salton Sea Fund	⊙ 432		.00
California Domestic Violence Victims Fund	⊙ 433		.00
Special Olympics Fund	⊙ 434		.00
Type 1 Diabetes Research Fund	⊙ 435		.00
California YMCA Youth and Government Voluntary Tax Contribution Fund	⊙ 436		.00
Habitat for Humanity Voluntary Tax Contribution Fund	⊙ 437		.00
California Senior Citizen Advocacy Voluntary Tax Contribution Fund	⊙ 438		.00
Native California Wildlife Rehabilitation Voluntary Tax Contribution Fund	⊙ 439		.00
Rape Backlog Kit Voluntary Tax Contribution Fund	⊙ 440		.00
110 Add code 400 through code 440. This is your total contribution	⊙ 110		.00

REV 00.0010 PRO
Side 4   Form 540 2017 | 175 | 3104174

31 | P a g e

Your name: [REDACTED]   Your SSN or ITIN: [REDACTED]

111 AMOUNT YOU OWE. If you do not have an amount on line 96, add line 93, line 97, and line 110. See instructions. Do not send cash.
Mail to: FRANCHISE TAX BOARD
PO BOX 942867
SACRAMENTO CA 94267-0001 .... ● **111** [   ] . 00
Pay online – Go to ftb.ca.gov/pay for more information.

112 Interest, late return penalties, and late payment penalties .... **112** [   ] . 00

113 Underpayment of estimated tax. Check the box: ● [ ] FTB 5805 attached ● [ ] FTB 5805F attached ● **113** [   ] . 00

114 Total amount due. See instructions. Enclose, but do not staple, any payment. .... **114** [   ] . 00

115 REFUND OR NO AMOUNT DUE. Subtract the sum of line 110, line 112 and line 113 from line 96. See instructions.
Mail to: FRANCHISE TAX BOARD
PO BOX 942840
SACRAMENTO CA 94240-0001 .... ● **115** [, 0] . 00

Fill in the information to authorize direct deposit of your refund into one or two accounts. Do not attach a voided check or a deposit slip. See instructions.
Have you verified the routing and account numbers? Use whole dollars only.
All or the following amount of my refund (line 115) is authorized for direct deposit into the account shown below:

● Type
● Routing number [   ] [ ] Checking ● Account number [   ] ● **116** Direct deposit amount [   ] . 00
[ ] Savings

The remaining amount of my refund (line 115) is authorized for direct deposit into the account shown below:

● Type
● Routing number [   ] [ ] Checking ● Account number [   ] ● **117** Direct deposit amount [   ] . 00
[ ] Savings

IMPORTANT: See the instructions to find out if you should attach a copy of your complete federal tax return.

To learn about your privacy rights, how we may use your information, and the consequences for not providing the requested information, go to ftb.ca.gov/forms and search for 1131. To request this notice by mail, call 800.852.5711. Under penalties of perjury, I declare that I have examined this tax return, including accompanying schedules and statements, and to the best of my knowledge and belief, it is true, correct, and complete.

Your signature	Date	Spouse's/RDP's signature (if a joint tax return, both must sign)

Sign Here

It is unlawful to forge a spouse's/RDP's signature.

Joint tax return? (See instructions)

◉ Your email address. Enter only one email address.
[   ]

◉ Preferred phone number
(9 , 4 , 9) 7 , 1 , 6 ◡ 7 , 9 , 4 , 9

Paid preparer's signature (declaration of preparer is based on all information of which preparer has any knowledge)
[   ]

Firm's name (or yours, if self-employed)
PROFESSIONAL FINANCIAL SERVICES

● PTIN
P , 0 , 1 , 5 , 1 , 3 , 0 , 0 , 2

Firm's address
151 KALMUS DR STE C210 COSTA MESA CA 92626

● FEIN
3 , 3 ◡ 0 , 8 , 9 , 1 , 1 , 8 , 9

Do you want to allow another person to discuss this tax return with us? See instructions... ● [ ] Yes ● [✗] No

Print Third Party Designee's Name
[   ]

Telephone Number
(   )

REV 01/24/18 PRO   175   3105174   Form 540 2017   Side 5

2017 California Adjustments — Residents

Important: Attach this schedule behind Form 540, Side 5 as a supporting California schedule.

Name(s) as shown on tax return

SSN or ITIN

Part I Income Adjustment Schedule

Section A – Income

		A Federal Amounts (taxable amounts from your federal tax return)	B Subtractions See Instructions	C Additions See Instructions
7	Wages, salaries, tips, etc. See instructions before making an entry in column B or C 7	918.		
8	Taxable interest (b)_____ . . . . 8(a)			
9	Ordinary dividends. See Instructions. (b)_____ . . . . 9(a)			
10	Taxable refunds, credits, offsets of state and local income taxes 10			
11	Alimony received 11			
12	Business income or (loss) 12	24,619.	381.	
13	Capital gain or (loss). See instructions. 13			
14	Other gains or (losses) 14			
15	IRA distributions. See Instructions. (a)_____ . . . . 15(b)			
16	Pensions and annuities. See Instructions. (a)_____ . . . . 16(b)			
17	Rental real estate, royalties, partnerships, S corporations, trusts, etc 17			
18	Farm income or (loss) 18			
19	Unemployment compensation 19			
20	Social security benefits (a) ○_____ . . . . 20(b)			
21	Other income.		a	a
	a California lottery winnings b NOL from FTB 3805Z,		b	b
	b Disaster loss deduction from FTB 3805V 3806, 3807, or 3809	21	c	c
	c Federal NOL (Form 1040, line 21) f Other (describe):		d	d
	d NOL deduction from FTB 3805V ○_____		e	e
			f	f
22	Total. Combine line 7 through line 21 in column A. Add line 7 through line 21 in column B and column C. Go to Section B. 22	25,537.	381.	

Section B – Adjustments to Income

23	Educator expenses 23			
24	Certain business expenses of reservists, performing artists, and fee-basis government officials 24			
25	Health savings account deduction 25			
26	Moving expenses 26			
27	Deductible part of self-employment tax 27	1,740.		
28	Self-employed SEP, SIMPLE, and qualified plans 28			
29	Self-employed health insurance deduction 29			
30	Penalty on early withdrawal of savings 30			
31a	Alimony paid. (b) Recipient's: SSN ○ ___ – ___ – ___			
	Last name ○_____ . . . 31a			
32	IRA deduction 32			
33	Student loan interest deduction 33			
34	Reserved 34			
35	Domestic production activities deduction 35			
36	Add line 23 through line 31a and line 32 through line 35 in columns A, B, and C. See instructions 36	1,740.		
37	Total. Subtract line 36 from line 22 in columns A, B, and C. See instructions 37	23,797.	381.	

REV 01/19/18 PRO

Part II   Adjustments to Federal Itemized Deductions

38	Federal itemized deductions. Enter the amount from federal Schedule A (Form 1040), lines 4, 9, 15, 19, 20, 27, and 28	⊙ 38	19,290.
39	Enter total of federal Schedule A (Form 1040), line 5 (State Disability Insurance, and state and local income tax, or General Sales Tax) and line 8 (foreign income taxes only). See instructions	⊙ 39	586.
40	Subtract line 39 from line 38	⊙ 40	18,704.
41	Other adjustments including California lottery losses. See instructions. Specify [ ]	⊙ 41	
42	Combine line 40 and line 41	⊙ 42	18,704.

43 Is your federal AGI (Form 540, line 13) more than the amount shown below for your filing status?

        Single or married/RDP filing separately $187,203

        Head of household $280,808

        Married/RDP filing jointly or qualifying widow(er) $374,411

    No. Transfer the amount on line 42 to line 43.

Yes. Complete the Itemized Deductions Worksheet in the instructions for Schedule CA (540), line 43	⊙ 43	18,704.

44 Enter the larger of the amount on line 43 or your standard deduction listed below .

        Single or married/RDP filing separately. See instructions $4,236

        Married/RDP filing jointly, head of household, or qualifying widow(er) $8,472

Transfer the amount on line 44 to Form 540, line 18	⊙ 44	18,704.

EXHIBIT '6':

Respondent's Certified Court Minutes (04HF1326)

MINUTES

Case : 04HF1326 F A

Name : ███████

Date of Action	Seq Nbr	Code	Text
09/01/04	1	FLDOC	Original Complaint filed on 09/01/2004 by Orange County District Attorney.
	2	FLCNT	FELONY charge of 496(a) PC filed as count 1. Date of violation: 08/27/2004.
	3	FLCNT	FELONY charge of 11377(a) HS filed as count 2. Date of violation: 08/27/2004.
	4	FLCNT	MISDEMEANOR charge of 11364 HS filed as count 3. Date of violation: 08/27/2004.
	5	FLCNT	MISDEMEANOR charge of 530.5(a) PC filed as count 4. Date of violation: 08/27/2004.
	6	CLADD	Case calendared on 09/01/04 at 1:30 PM in H2 for ARGN.
	7	FIFCI	Declaration/Affidavit in Support of Arrest filed.
	8	HHELD	Hearing held on 09/01/2004 at 01:30:00 PM in Department H2 for Arraignment.
	9	OFJUD	Officiating Judge: Craig E. Robison, Judge
	10	OFJA	Clerk: L. K. Mc Donald
	11	OFBAL	Bailiff: G. J. Van Patten
	12	OFREP	Court Reporter: Karen Lee
	13	APDDA	People represented by Yvette Patko, Deputy District Attorney, present.
	14	APDPP	Defendant present in Court in propria persona.
	15	DFTNC	Defendant states true name and date of birth are correct as shown on the complaint.
	16	APDPD	Court appoints Public Defender to represent Defendant.
	17	APDWPD	Defendant present in Court with counsel Michael Mc Clellan, Public Defender.
	18	CPACK	Counsel acknowledges receipt of the complaint.
	19	WVRAA	Defendant waives reading and advisement of the Original Complaint.
	20	PLNGA	To the Original Complaint defendant pleads NOT GUILTY to all counts.
	21	CLSET	Pre Trial set on 09/08/2004 at 08:30 AM in Department H2.
	22	CLSET	Preliminary Hearing set on 09/15/2004 at 08:30 AM in Department H2.

MINUTES

Case : 04HF1326 F A

Name : ▮▮▮▮▮▮▮▮▮▮

Date of Action	Seq Nbr	Code	Text
09/01/04	23	DFOTR	Defendant ordered to appear.
	24	BLSET	Court orders bail set in the amount of $25, 000.00.
	25	DFREM	Defendant remanded to the custody of the Sheriff.
	26	NTJAL	**Notice to Sheriff issued.**
	27	FIFPC	Fingerprint card is received and filed.
	28	TXKPW	Keep with companion cases(s) 04HM01441, 02HM02571.
09/08/04	1	HHELD	**Hearing held on 09/08/2004 at 08:30:00 AM in Department H2 for Pre Trial.**
	2	OFJUD	Officiating Judge: Craig E. Robison, Judge
	3	OFJA	Clerk: L. K. Mc Donald
	4	OFBAL	Bailiff: D. Cheli
	5	OFREP	Court Reporter: Karen Lee
	6	APDDA	People represented by Yvette Patko, Deputy District Attorney, present.
	7	APNDC	Defendant not present in Court represented by Michael Mc Clellan, Public Defender.
	8	APDHC	Defendant remains in holding cell, not brought into courtroom.
	9	CLCON	**Pre Trial continued to 09/13/2004 at 08:30 AM in Department H2 by stipulation of all parties.**
	10	CLTRM	**Preliminary Hearing for 09/15/2004 08:30 AM in H2 to remain.**
	11	BLSTR	Current bail set for defendant to remain.
	12	NTJAL	**Notice to Sheriff issued.**
	13	TXKPW	Keep with companion cases(s) 04HM01441, 02HM02571 & 03SF0869.
09/13/04	1	HHELD	**Hearing held on 09/13/2004 at 08:30:00 AM in Department H2 for Pre Trial.**
	2	OFJUD	Officiating Judge: Thomas Rees, Commissioner
	3	OFJA	Clerk: R. M. Hume
	4	OFBAL	Bailiff:. Present
	5	OFREP	Court Reporter: Karen Lee
	6	APDDA	People represented by Yvette Patko, Deputy District Attorney, present.

MINUTES

Case : 04HF1326 F A

Name : ▇▇▇▇▇▇▇

Date of Action	Seq Nbr	Code	Text
09/13/04	7	APNDC	Defendant not present in Court represented by Michael Mc Clellan, Public Defender.
	8	APDHC	Defendant remains in holding cell, not brought into courtroom.
	9	CLPTP	**Pretrial off calendar, Preliminary Hearing set on 09/15/2004 at 08:30 AM in H2 to remain.**
	10	BLSTR	Current bail set for defendant to remain.
	11	NTJAL	**Notice to Sheriff issued.**
	12	TXKPW	Keep with companion cases(s) 03SF0869, 04HM01441 & 02HM02571.
09/15/04	1	HHELD	**Hearing held on 09/15/2004 at 08:30:00 AM in Department H2 for Preliminary Hearing.**
	2	OFJUD	Officiating Judge: Craig E. Robison, Judge
	3	OFJA	Clerk: L. K. Mc Donald
	4	OFBAL	Bailiff: D. Cheli
	5	OFREP	Court Reporter: Karen Lee
	6	APDDA	People represented by Yvette Patko, Deputy District Attorney, present.
	7	APDWPD	Defendant present in Court with counsel Michael Mc Clellan, Public Defender.
	8	FIAMD	**First Amended Complaint filed by Orange County District Attorney.**
	9	CTAMC	To the First Amended Complaint count 1 now reads 496(a) PC, FELONY. Date of violation: 05/01/2004.
	10	CTAMC	To the First Amended Complaint count 4 now reads 530.5(a) PC, FELONY. Date of violation: 05/01/2004.
	11	CTADD	First Amended Complaint now charges COUNT 5, 496(a) PC, FELONY, date of violation 07/12/2004.
	12	CTADD	First Amended Complaint now charges COUNT 6, 530.5(a) PC, FELONY, date of violation 07/12/2004.
	13	CTADD	First Amended Complaint now charges COUNT 7, 496(a) PC, FELONY, date of violation 08/22/2004.
	14	CTADD	First Amended Complaint now charges COUNT 8, 530.5(a) PC, FELONY, date of violation 08/22/2004.
	15	CTADD	First Amended Complaint now charges COUNT 9, 496(a) PC, FELONY, date of violation 07/15/2004.

MINUTES

Case : 04HF1326 F A

Name : ███████████

Date of Action	Seq Nbr	Code	Text
09/15/04	16	CTADD	First Amended Complaint now charges COUNT 10, 530.5(a) PC, FELONY, date of violation 07/15/2004.
	17	CTADD	First Amended Complaint now charges COUNT 11, 496(a) PC, FELONY, date of violation 08/27/2004.
	18	CTADD	First Amended Complaint now charges COUNT 12, 530.5(a) PC, FELONY, date of violation 08/27/2004.
	19	CTADD	First Amended Complaint now charges COUNT 13, 496(a) PC, FELONY, date of violation 08/27/2004.
	20	CTADD	First Amended Complaint now charges COUNT 14, 530.5(a) PC, FELONY, date of violation 08/27/2004.
	21	CTADD	First Amended Complaint now charges COUNT 15, 496(a) PC, FELONY, date of violation 08/27/2004.
	22	CTADD	First Amended Complaint now charges COUNT 16, 530.5(a) PC, FELONY, date of violation 08/27/2004.
	23	CTADD	First Amended Complaint now charges COUNT 17, 496(a) PC, FELONY, date of violation 08/27/2004.
	24	CTADD	First Amended Complaint now charges COUNT 18, 530.5(a) PC, FELONY, date of violation 08/27/2004.
	25	CTADD	First Amended Complaint now charges COUNT 19, 496(a) PC, FELONY, date of violation 08/27/2004.
	26	CTADD	First Amended Complaint now charges COUNT 20, 530.5(a) PC, FELONY, date of violation 08/27/2004.
	27	CTADD	First Amended Complaint now charges COUNT 21, 496(a) PC, FELONY, date of violation 08/27/2004.
	28	CTADD	First Amended Complaint now charges COUNT 22, 530.5(a) PC, FELONY, date of violation 08/27/2004.
	29	CPACK	Counsel acknowledges receipt of the complaint.
	30	WVRAA	Defendant waives reading and advisement of the First Amended Complaint.
	31	CLSET	**Arraignment set on 09/17/2004 at 08:30 AM in Department H2.**
	32	CLTXT	**re: arraignment on 1st amended complaint**
	33	WVRAT	Defendant waives the right to be arraigned today.
	34	WVTPH	Court finds the defendant understandingly, knowingly, and voluntarily waives the right to a Preliminary Hearing within 10 court days of arraignment.
	35	PLCJN	Counsel joins in waivers.

MINUTES

Case : 04HF1326 F A

Name : Ashaary, Kiarash

Date of Action	Seq Nbr	Code	Text
09/15/04	36	DFOTR	Defendant ordered to appear.
	37	BLSTR	Current bail set for defendant to remain.
	38	DFREM	Defendant remanded to the custody of the Sheriff.
	39	NTJAL	**Notice to Sheriff issued.**
	40	TXKPW	Keep with companion cases(s) 03SF0869, 04HM01441, 02HM02571.
09/17/04	1	HHELD	**Hearing held on 09/17/2004 at 08:30:00 AM in Department H2 for Arraignment.**
	2	OFJUD	Officiating Judge: Craig E. Robison, Judge
	3	OFJA	Clerk: L. K. Mc Donald
	4	OFBAL	Bailiff: D. Cheli
	5	OFREP	Court Reporter: Karen Lee
	6	APDDA	People represented by Sandra Nassar, Deputy District Attorney, present.
	7	APDWPD	Defendant present in Court with counsel Michael Mc Clellan, Public Defender.
	8	APSUB	Robert M Brodney, Retained Attorney, substituting in as Attorney of Record.
	9	APATR	Michael Mc Clellan relieved as Counsel of Record.
	10	APDWRA	Defendant present in Court with counsel Brodney, Robert M, Retained Attorney.
	11	CPACK	Counsel acknowledges receipt of the complaint.
	12	WVRAA	Defendant waives reading and advisement of the First Amended Complaint.
	13	PLNGA	**To the First Amended Complaint defendant pleads NOT GUILTY to all counts.**
	14	CLSET	**Pre Trial set on 10/20/2004 at 08:30 AM in Department H2.**
	15	CLSET	**Preliminary Hearing set on 11/09/2004 at 08:30 AM in Department H2.**
	16	WVTPH	Court finds the defendant understandingly, knowingly, and voluntarily waives the right to a Preliminary Hearing within 10 court days/60 calendar days of arraignment.
	17	PLCJN	Counsel joins in waivers.
	18	DFOTR	Defendant ordered to appear.
	19	BLSTR	Current bail set for defendant to remain.

Name:

Page 5 of 16

MINUTES / ALL CATEGORIES

Case: 04HF1326 F A

2/19/19 2:06 pm

40 | Page

MINUTES

Case : 04HF1326 F A

Name : ███████████

Date of Action	Seq Nbr	Code	Text
09/17/04	20	DFREM	Defendant remanded to the custody of the Sheriff.
	21	NTJAL	**Notice to Sheriff issued.**
	22	TXKPW	Keep with companion cases(s) 03SF0869, 04HM01441, 02HM02571.
09/23/04	1	CLADD	**Case calendared on 09/23/04 at 10:00 AM in H2 for HRG.**
	2	HHELD	**Hearing held on 09/23/2004 at 10:00:00 AM in Department H2 for Hearing.**
	3	OFJUD	Officiating Judge: Craig E. Robison, Judge
	4	OFJA	Clerk: L. K. Mc Donald
	5	OFBAL	Bailiff: D. Cheli
	6	OFREP	Court Reporter: Karen Lee
	7	APDDA	People represented by Joe Williams, Deputy District Attorney, present.
	8	APNDC	Defendant not present in Court represented by Robert M Brodney, Retained Attorney.
	9	FIORD	Order to allow visitation for interview purposes signed and filed.
	10	TEXT	(Order filed in case number 04HF1326)
	11	CLTRM	**Pre Trial for 10/20/2004 08:30 AM in H2 to remain.**
	12	CLTRM	**Preliminary Hearing for 11/09/2004 08:30 AM in H2 to remain.**
	13	CPGTO	Certified Copy of order given to counsel.
	14	CPGTO	Certified Copy of Order forwarded to OCJ.
10/20/04	1	HHELD	**Hearing held on 10/20/2004 at 08:30:00 AM in Department H2 for Pre Trial.**
	2	OFJUD	Officiating Judge: Craig E. Robison, Judge
	3	OFJA	Clerk: L. K. Mc Donald
	4	OFBAL	Bailiff: D. Cheli
	5	OFREP	Court Reporter: Karen Lee
	6	APDDA	People represented by Yvette Patko, Deputy District Attorney, present.
	7	APDWRA	Defendant present in Court with counsel Brodney, Robert M, Retained Attorney.

Name: ███████████

Page 6 of 16

MINUTES / ALL CATEGORIES

Case: 04HF1326 F A

2/19/19 2:06 pm 37

41 | P a g e

MINUTES

Case : 04HF1326 F A

Name : ███████

Date of Action	Seq Nbr	Code	Text
10/20/04	8	CLVAC	Preliminary Hearing vacated for 11/09/2004 at 08:30 AM in H2.
	9	CLCON	Pre Trial continued to 11/15/2004 at 08:30 AM in Department H2 at request of Defense.
	10	WVTPH	Court finds the defendant understandingly, knowingly, and voluntarily waives the right to a Preliminary Hearing within 60 calendar days of arraignment.
	11	PLCJN	Counsel joins in waivers.
	12	DFOTR	Defendant ordered to appear.
	13	BLSTR	Current bail set for defendant to remain.
	14	DFREM	Defendant remanded to the custody of the Sheriff.
	15	NTJAL	**Notice to Sheriff issued.**
	16	TXKPW	Keep with companion cases(s) 03SF0869, 04HM01441, 02HM02571.
11/15/04	1	HHELD	Hearing held on 11/15/2004 at 08:30:00 AM in Department H2 for Pre Trial.
	2	OFJUD	Officiating Judge: Craig E. Robison, Judge
	3	OFJA	Clerk: L. K. Mc Donald
	4	OFBAL	Bailiff: D. Cheli
	5	OFREP	Court Reporter: Tina O'Rourke
	6	APDDA	People represented by Yvette Patko, Deputy District Attorney, present.
	7	APDWRA	Defendant present in Court with counsel Brodney, Robert M, Retained Attorney.
	8	CLCON	Pre Trial continued to 12/02/2004 at 08:30 AM in Department H2 at request of Defense.
	9	WVTPH	Court finds the defendant understandingly, knowingly, and voluntarily waives the right to a Preliminary Hearing within 60 calendar days of arraignment.
	10	PLCJN	Counsel joins in waivers.
	11	DFOTR	Defendant ordered to appear.
	12	BLSTR	Current bail set for defendant to remain.
	13	DFREM	Defendant remanded to the custody of the Sheriff.
	14	NTJAL	**Notice to Sheriff issued.**
	15	TXKPW	Keep with companion cases(s) 03SF0869, 04HM01441, 02HM02571.

MINUTES

Case : 04HF1326 F A

Name : ████████████

Date of Action	Seq Nbr	Code	Text
12/02/04	1	HHELD	Hearing held on 12/02/2004 at 08:30:00 AM in Department H2 for Pre Trial.
	2	OFJUD	Officiating Judge: Craig E. Robison, Judge
	3	OFJA	Clerk: L. K. Mc Donald
	4	OFBAL	Bailiff: D. Cheli
	5	OFREP	Court Reporter: Karen Lee
	6	APSDA	Joe Williams made a special appearance for District Attorney Yvette Patko.
	7	APDWRA	Defendant present in Court with counsel Brodney, Robert M, Retained Attorney.
	8	ADLCR	Defendant advised of legal and constitutional rights.
	9	ADCZS	Defendant advised of the possible consequences of plea affecting deportation and citizenship.
	10	ADMAX	Defendant advised of maximum possible sentence.
	11	ADCSQ	Defendant advised of consequences of violating probation and parole.
	12	PLWTH	**Defendant's motion to WITHDRAW NOT GUILTY PLEA to count(s) 2, 4, 6, 8, 10, 11, 14, 16, 17, 20, 22 granted.**
	13	PLGCT	**To the First Amended Complaint defendant pleads GUILTY as to count(s) 2, 4, 6, 8, 10, 11, 14, 16, 17, 20, 22.**
	14	PLFWR	Court finds defendant intelligently and voluntarily waives legal and constitutional rights to jury trial, confront and examine witnesses, and to remain silent.
	15	PLFBA	Court finds factual basis and accepts plea.
	16	FIWWR	Defendant's written waiver of legal and constitutional rights for guilty plea received and ordered filed.
	17	CLSET	**Sentencing set on 12/23/2004 at 08:30 AM in Department H2.**
	18	WVTIM	Defendant waives statutory time for Sentencing.
	19	PLCJN	Counsel joins in waivers.
	20	TEXT	If restitution is paid in full by 12/23/2004, then defendant to receive probation sentence. If not, defendant to receive State Prison sentence)
	21	DFOTR	Defendant ordered to appear.
	22	BLSTR	Current bail set for defendant to remain.

43 | P a g e

SUPERIOR COURT OF THE STATE OF CALIFORNIA,
COUNTY OF ORANGE

MINUTES

Case : 04HF1326 F A

Name : ▓▓▓▓▓▓▓▓▓▓▓

Date of Action	Seq Nbr	Code	Text
12/02/04	23	DFREM	Defendant remanded to the custody of the Sheriff.
	24	NTJAL	**Notice to Sheriff issued.**
	25	TXKPW	Keep with companion cases(s) 03SF1326, 04HM01441, 02HM02571.
12/23/04	1	HHELD	**Hearing held on 12/23/2004 at 08:30:00 AM in Department H2 for Sentencing.**
	2	OFJUD	Officiating Judge: James Odriozola, Commissioner
	3	OFJA	Clerk: A. T. Akahoshi
	4	OFBAL	Bailiff: L. Trebil
	5	OFREP	Court Reporter: Karen Lee
	6	APDDA	People represented by Yvette Patko, Deputy District Attorney, present.
	7	APDWC	Defendant present in Court with counsel Robert M Brodney, Retained Attorney.
	8	DFSTC	All Parties being advised of their right to have this matter heard by a Judge of the court have stipulated that the matter be heard by Commissioner James Odriozola.
	9	WVAFS	Defendant waives arraignment for sentencing.
	10	PBDAP	Defendant applies for probation.
	11	WVPBR	Probation report waived.
	12	CDCDM	Count(s) 1, 3, 5, 7, 9, 12, 13, 15, 18, 19, 21 DISMISSED - Motion of People.
	13	PRISS	No legal cause why judgment should not be pronounced and defendant having Pled Guilty to count(s) 2, 4, 6, 8, 10, 11, 14, 16, 17, 20, 22, Imposition of sentence is suspended and defendant is placed on 3 Years FORMAL PROBATION on the following terms and conditions:
	14	PRJAL	**Serve 180 Day(s) Orange County Jail as to count(s) 2, 4, 6, 8, 10, 11, 14, 16, 17, 20, 22.**
	15	JLCTS	**Credit for time served: 119 actual, 60 conduct, totaling 179 days.**
	16	PRSRF	Pay $200.00 Restitution Fine pursuant to Penal Code 1202.4 or Penal Code 1202.4(b).
	17	PRHAR	Defendant is ordered to make restitution on dismissed count(s) 1, 3, 5, 7, 9, 12, 13, 15, 18, 19, 21 pursuant to Harvey Waiver.

MINUTES

Case : 04HF1326 F A

Name :

Date of Action	Seq Nbr	Code	Text
12/23/04	18	PRRES	Pay restitution in the amount as determined and directed by Probation Officer as to count(s) 2, 4, 6, 8, 10, 11, 14, 16, 17, 20, 22.
	19	ADRDH	Defendant advised of the right to have the amount of restitution determined by a Judicial Bench Officer after a formal hearing.
	20	PRRIL	Court orders 10% interest of judgment from date of loss.
	21	PRRDC	The restitution ordered on 12/23/2004 is deemed a civil judgment pursuant to Penal Code Section 1214(b) as to count(s) 2, 4, 6, 8, 10, 11, 14, 16, 17, 20, 22.
	22	PRREG	Register pursuant to Health & Safety Code 11590.
	23	PRFLA	Pay $50.00 Controlled Substance Lab FEE pursuant to Health and Safety Code Section 11372.5.
	24	PRFEP	All fees payable through the Probation Department.
	25	PRNUD	Use no unauthorized drugs, narcotics, or controlled substances. Submit to drug or narcotic testing as directed by Probation Officer or Police Officer.
	26	PRSAS	Submit your person and property including any residence, premises, container, or vehicle under your control to search and seizure at any time of the day or night by any law enforcement or probation officer with or without a warrant, and with or without reasonable cause or reasonable suspicion.
	27	PRPSY	Cooperate with Probation Officer in any plan for psychiatric, psychological, alcohol and/or drug treatment, or counseling.
	28	PRNCC	Have no blank checks in possession, nor write any portion of any checks, nor have checking account, nor use or possess credit cards or open credit accounts unless approved by Probation.
	29	PRTSE	Seek training, schooling, or employment and maintain residence as approved by Probation Department.
	30	PRASA	Do not associate with anyone disapproved of by your Probation Officer.
	31	PRNWP	Do not own, use, or possess any type of dangerous or deadly weapon.
	32	DFCPP	Defendant provided a copy of "Prohibited Persons Notice Form and Power of Attorney for Firearms and Disposal" pursuant to Penal Code 12021(d)(2).

MINUTES

Case : 04HF1326 F A

Name : ███████████

Date of Action	Seq Nbr	Code	Text
12/23/04	33	PROBY	Obey all laws, orders, rules, and regulations of the Court, Jail, and Probation.
	34	PRVNL	Violate no law.
	35	PRNOC	Do not have any contact with Gregory Kaltenbach, Candace Wengert, Donald Seward, Donna Colema, John Richmond, Judith Brown Gibbs, Mildred Wynne, Douglas Mahaffey, Shirley Smith, Liliuana Nuila and Meghan McClain directly, indirectly, or through a third party except by an Attorney of Record.
	36	PRATC	Defendant accepts terms and conditions of probation.
	37	PRCTP	All terms and conditions to be directed and monitored through the Probation Department.
	38	PRTXT	Defendant to report to Probation Office upon release from custody by Monday, December 27, 2004, at 5:00 p.m.
	39	PRPCD	Pay the costs of probation based on the ability to pay as directed by the Probation Officer.
	40	DFREM	Defendant remanded to the custody of the Sheriff.
	41	NTJAL	**Notice to Sheriff issued.**
	42	NTPRT	Probation Order printed.
12/27/04	1	DMABS	DD1-GJZ sent to DMV. Return Code: 800
12/31/04	1	DOJABS	DOJ Initial Abstract sent.
02/18/05	1	CLADD	**Case calendared on 02/18/05 at 08:30 AM in H2 for MTN MOP.**
	2	CLCAN	MTN MOP set on 02/18/05 at 08:30 AM in H2 has been cancelled.
09/22/05	1	HHELD	**Hearing held on 09/22/2005 at 08:30 AM in Department C5 for Chambers Work.**
	2	OFJUD	Officiating Judge: Richard F. Toohey, Judge
	3	OFJA	Clerk: M. Alcaraz
	4	APNCR	No Court Reporter present at proceedings.
	5	APTXT	No appearance
	6	FITXT	Petition for Warrant of Arrest signed and filed.
	7	PBREV	Probation ordered revoked as to count(s) 2, 4, 6, 8, 10, 11, 14, 16, 17, 20, 22.
	8	WAISD	Bench warrant ordered issued for defendant. Bail set at $0.00, NO BAIL.

MINUTES

Case : 04HF1326 F A

Name : ███████████

Date of Action	Seq Nbr	Code	Text
09/27/05	1	WAWSD	Bench warrant signed by Richard F. Toohey and issued for defendant. Bail set at $0.00, NO BAIL.
09/28/05	1	WFNBR	Warrant File Number 02924708 sent from AWSS for Warrant # 2216368.
02/08/06	1	WASVD	Warrant 02924708 for Kiarash Ashaary DEFENDANT served by Irvine Police Department on 02/08/2006.
02/09/06	1	CLCST2	**Probation Violation re: Arraignment - In Custody set on 02/09/2006 at 09:00 AM in Department C5.**
	2	HHELD	**Hearing held on 02/09/2006 at 09:00:00 AM in Department C5 for Probation Violation Arraignment - In Custody.**
	3	OFNOC	# 103 on calendar.
	4	OFJUD	Officiating Judge: Kazuharu Makino, Judge
	5	OFJA	Clerk: L. Torres
	6	OFBAL	Bailiff: R. P. Holt
	7	OFREP	Court Reporter: Caryl Axton
	8	WAREC	Warrant issued on 09/27/2005 ordered recalled for defendant.
	9	APDWPD	Defendant present in Court with counsel James Steinberg, Public Defender.
	10	APDDA	People represented by Gary Logalbo, Deputy District Attorney, present.
	11	CLCON2	**Probation Violation re: Arraignment - In Custody continued to 02/23/2006 at 09:00 AM in Department C5 by stipulation of all parties.**
	12	DFOTR	Defendant ordered to appear.
	13	BLNOB	Court orders bail set at NO BAIL.
	14	DFREM	Defendant remanded to the custody of the Sheriff.
	15	NTJAL	**Notice to Sheriff issued.**
	16	OFMEC	Minutes entered by S. Young.
02/23/06	1	HHELD	**Hearing held on 02/23/2006 at 09:00:00 AM in Department C5 for Probation Violation Arraignment - In Custody.**
	2	OFJUD	Officiating Judge: Kazuharu Makino, Judge
	3	OFJA	Clerk: L. Torres
	4	OFBAL	Bailiff: R. P. Holt

MINUTES

Case : 04HF1326 F A

Name :

Date of Action	Seq Nbr	Code	Text
02/23/06	5	OFREP	Court Reporter: Colleen Flynn
	6	OFNOC	# 30 on calendar.
	7	APDWRA	Defendant present in Court with counsel Brodney, Robert M, Retained Attorney.
	8	APDDA	People represented by Gary Logalbo, Deputy District Attorney, present.
	9	APSUB	Robert M Brodney, Retained Attorney, substituting in as Attorney of Record.
	10	APATR	James Steinberg relieved as Counsel of Record.
	11	CLCON2	**Probation Violation re: Arraignment - In Custody continued to 03/23/2006 at 09:00 AM in Department C5 at request of Defense.**
	12	DFOTR	Defendant ordered to return.
	13	DFREM	Defendant remanded to the custody of the Sheriff.
	14	BLSTR	Current bail set for defendant to remain.
	15	NTJAL	**Notice to Sheriff issued.**
	16	TXKPW	Keep with companion cases(s) 03SF0869.
	17	OFMEC	Minutes entered by C. Anderson.
03/23/06	1	HHELD	**Hearing held on 03/23/2006 at 09:00:00 AM in Department C5 for Probation Violation Arraignment - In Custody.**
	2	OFJUD	Officiating Judge: Kazuharu Makino, Judge
	3	OFJA	Clerk: L. Torres
	4	OFBAL	Bailiff: R. P. Holt
	5	OFREP	Court Reporter: Colleen Flynn
	6	OFNOC	# 29 on calendar.
	7	APDWRA	Defendant present in Court with counsel Brodney, Robert M, Retained Attorney.
	8	APDDA	People represented by Andrew Haughton, Deputy District Attorney, present.
	9	WVTIM	Defendant waives statutory time for Probation Violation.
	10	PLCJN	Counsel joins in waivers.
	11	CLCON2	**Probation Violation re: Arraignment - In Custody continued to 04/10/2006 at 09:00 AM in Department C5 at request of Defense.**

MINUTES

Case : 04HF1326 F A

Name : ▮▮▮▮▮▮▮▮▮▮

Date of Action	Seq Nbr	Code	Text
03/23/06	12	DFOTR	Defendant ordered to return.
	13	DFREM	Defendant remanded to the custody of the Sheriff.
	14	BLSTR	Current bail set for defendant to remain.
	15	NTJAL	**Notice to Sheriff issued.**
	16	TXKPW	Keep with companion cases(s) 03SF0869.
	17	OFMEC	Minutes entered by C. Anderson.
04/10/06	1	HHELD	**Hearing held on 04/10/2006 at 09:00:00 AM in Department C5 for Probation Violation Arraignment - In Custody.**
	2	OFJUD	Officiating Judge: Kazuharu Makino, Judge
	3	OFJA	Clerk: L. Torres
	4	OFBAL	Bailiff: C. J. Thurber
	5	OFREP	Court Reporter: Colleen Flynn
	6	OFNOC	# 22 on calendar.
	7	APDWRA	Defendant present in Court with counsel Brodney, Robert M, Retained Attorney.
	8	APDDA	People represented by Daniel Wagner, Deputy District Attorney, present.
	9	CLCON2	**Probation Violation re: Arraignment - In Custody continued to 05/25/2006 at 09:00 AM in Department C5 at request of Defense.**
	10	DFOTR	Defendant ordered to return.
	11	DFREM	Defendant remanded to the custody of the Sheriff.
	12	BLSTR	Current bail set for defendant to remain.
	13	NTJAL	**Notice to Sheriff issued.**
	14	TXKPW	Keep with companion cases(s) 03SF0869.
	15	OFMEC	Minutes entered by C. Anderson.
05/25/06	1	HHELD	**Hearing held on 05/25/2006 at 09:00:00 AM in Department C5 for Probation Violation Arraignment - In Custody.**
	2	OFJUD	Officiating Judge: Kazuharu Makino, Judge
	3	OFJA	Clerk: L. Torres
	4	OFBAL	Bailiff: C. J. Thurber
	5	OFREP	Court Reporter: Shelley Hill

MINUTES

Case : 04HF1326 F A

Name : ███████████

Date of Action	Seq Nbr	Code	Text
05/25/06	6	OFNOC	# 15 on calendar.
	7	APDWRA	Defendant present in Court with counsel Brodney, Robert M, Retained Attorney.
	8	APDDA	People represented by Andre Manssourian, Deputy District Attorney, present.
	9	ADLCR	Defendant advised of legal and constitutional rights.
	10	PBADV	Defendant waives right to probation hearing. Defendant admits violation of probation as to count(s) 2, 4, 6, 8, 10, 11, 14, 16, 17, 20, 22.
	11	FDCVP	Court finds defendant in violation of probation.
	12	WVPBR	Probation report waived.
	13	WVAFS	Defendant waives arraignment for sentencing.
	14	PLRIS	Defendant requests immediate sentencing.
	15	PLCJN	Counsel joins in waivers and admissions.
	16	PBRSM	Court orders probation reinstated and modified as to count(s) 2, 4, 6, 8, 10, 11, 14, 16, 17, 20, 22 as follows:
	17	PBTRM	Court orders probation terminated as to count(s) 2, 4, 6, 8, 10, 11, 14, 16, 17, 20, 22.
	18	NTRCO	Defendant released on this case only. Release issued.
	19	NTJAL	**Notice to Sheriff issued.**
	20	OFMEC	Minutes entered by C. Anderson.
05/29/06	1	DOJABS	DOJ Subsequent Abstract sent.
12/08/06	1	CPGTO	Certified Copy of prior packet forwarded to Orange County District Attorney's Office, N. Adams.
09/28/07	1	PRLINK	Transferred from: Ashaary, Kiarash
09/20/08	1	CSCLS	**Case closed.**
11/30/18	1	CLADD	**At the request of Defense Counsel, case calendared on 11/30/18 at 08:30 AM in C53 for PET.**
	2	HHELD	**Hearing held on 11/30/2018 at 08:30:00 AM in Department C53 for Petition.**
	3	OFJUD	Judicial Officer: Gary M Pohlson, Judge
	4	OFJA	Clerk: N. Robles
	5	OFBAL	Bailiff: E. F. Richardson
	6	OFREP	Court Reporter: Shelley Hill

MINUTES

Case : 04HF1326 F A

Name : ███████████

Date of Action	Seq Nbr	Code	Text
11/30/18	7	APDDA	People represented by George William McFetridge Jr, Deputy District Attorney, present.
	8	APNDC	Defendant not present in Court represented by Saif Rahman, Retained Attorney.
	9	FIMTN	Defense Motion to Withdraw Plea Pursuant to Penal Code 1473.7 filed.
	10	CORAC	Court read and considered Petition for Relief Under Penal Code 1473.7.
	11	TRPRS	People submit(s).
	12	MOTION	Motion granted.
	13	FDTXT	Court finds the defendant was not advised of their immigration consequences and grants the motion pursuant to Penal Code 1473.7. The defendant withdraws his guilty plea(s). People state they are unable to proceed at this time. Defense requests the Court dismiss this case in the furtherance of justice. The Court orders this case dismissed pursuant to Penal Code 1385.
	14	PLWTH	**Defendant's motion to WITHDRAW GUILTY PLEA to count(s) 2, 4, 6, 8, 10, 11, 14, 16, 17, 20, 22 granted.**
	16	CDCAS	Case dismissed - pursuant to Penal Code 1385 - Furtherance of justice.
	17	FIORD	Order Vacating Conviction Under Penal Code 1473.7 signed and filed.
	18	OFMDD	Minutes of 11/30/2018 entered on 12/03/2018.
12/03/18	1	DOJABS	DOJ Correction Abstract sent.
12/05/18	1	FXDMVA	Deleted DD1 - Abstract of Conviction abstract from case.
12/06/18	1	CSCLS	**Case closed.**

Name ███████

Page 16 of 16

MINUTES / ALL CATEGORIES

Case: 04HF1326 F A

2/19/19 2:06 pm

51 | Page

EXHIBIT '7':

Respondent's Certified Court Minutes (06HF2202)

MINUTES

Case : 06HF2202 F A

Name : █████████

Date of Action	Seq Nbr	Code	Text
11/07/06	1	FLDOC	Original Complaint filed on 11/07/2006 by Orange County District Attorney.
	2	FLNAM	Name filed: Ashaary, Kiarash
	3	FLCNT	FELONY charge of 530.5(a) PC filed as count 1. Date of violation: 12/26/2005.
	4	FLCNT	FELONY charge of 530.5(a) PC filed as count 2. Date of violation: 01/30/2006.
	5	FLCNT	FELONY charge of 530.5(a) PC filed as count 3. Date of violation: 02/05/2006.
	6	FLCNT	FELONY charge of 530.5(a) PC filed as count 4. Date of violation: 01/28/2006.
	7	FLCNT	FELONY charge of 530.5(a) PC filed as count 5. Date of violation: 01/24/2006.
	8	FLCNT	FELONY charge of 530.5(a) PC filed as count 6. Date of violation: 01/25/2006.
	9	FLCNT	FELONY charge of 530.5(a) PC filed as count 7. Date of violation: 12/06/2005.
	10	FLCNT	FELONY charge of 530.5(a) PC filed as count 8. Date of violation: 01/04/2006.
	11	FLCNT	FELONY charge of 530.5(a) PC filed as count 9. Date of violation: 11/27/2005.
	12	FLCNT	FELONY charge of 530.5(a) PC filed as count 10. Date of violation: 02/02/2006.
	13	FLCNT	FELONY charge of 530.5(a) PC filed as count 11. Date of violation: 02/08/2006.
	14	FLCNT	FELONY charge of 530.5(a) PC filed as count 12. Date of violation: 10/27/2005.
	15	FLCNT	FELONY charge of 459-460(b) PC filed as count 13. Date of violation: 10/17/2005.
	16	FLCNT	FELONY charge of 115(a) PC filed as count 14. Date of violation: 02/08/2006.
	17	FLCNT	FELONY charge of 470a PC filed as count 15. Date of violation: 02/08/2006.
	18	FLCNT	FELONY charge of 470b PC filed as count 16. Date of violation: 02/08/2006.
	19	FLCNT	MISDEMEANOR charge of 529.5(a) PC filed as count 17. Date of violation: 02/08/2006.

SUPERIOR COURT OF THE STATE OF CALIFORNIA, COUNTY OF ORANGE

MINUTES

Case : 06HF2202 F A
Name : Ashaary, Kiarash

Date of Action	Seq Nbr	Code	Text
11/07/06	20	FLCNT	FELONY charge of 475(b) PC filed as count 18. Date of violation: 02/08/2006.
	21	FLCNT	FELONY charge of 476 PC filed as count 19. Date of violation: 10/24/2005.
	22	FLALG	529.5(d) PC added as other allegation as to count 17.
	23	FLALG	13202.5(a) VC added as other allegation as to count 17.
	24	FIFCI	Declaration/Affidavit in Support of Arrest filed.
	25	FIFCI	Police/Arrest Report filed.
	26	TXBKF	Request for booking fees received.
	27	WAARS	Felony Warrant of Arrest requested.
	28	WAWSD	Warrant of Arrest warrant signed by Peter J. Polos and issued for defendant. Bail set at $100, 000.00, Mandatory Appearance.
	29	WAFAX	Warrant faxed to Central Warrant Repository (CWR).
	30	WFNBR	Warrant File Number 03006452 sent from AWSS for Warrant # 2303379.
11/20/06	1	WASVD	Warrant 03006452 for Kiarash Ashaary DEFENDANT served by Irvine Police Department on 11/20/2006.
11/22/06	1	CLADD	**Case calendared on 11/22/06 at 1:30 PM in H2 for ARGN IC.**
	2	HHELD	**Hearing held on 11/22/2006 at 01:30:00 PM in Department H2 for Arraignment In Custody.**
	3	OFJUD	Officiating Judge: Peter J. Polos, Judge
	4	OFJA	Clerk: C. B. Henderson
	5	OFBAL	Bailiff: J. Winovich
	6	OFREP	Court Reporter: Marcia Gahring
	7	WAREC	Warrant issued on 11/07/2006 ordered recalled for defendant.
	8	APDDA	People represented by Matthew Zandi, Deputy District Attorney, present.
	9	APDWC	Defendant present in Court with counsel Robert M Brodney, Retained Attorney.
	10	DFTNC	Defendant states true name and date of birth are correct as shown on the complaint.
	11	CPACK	Counsel acknowledges receipt of the complaint.

Case : 06HF2202 F A

Name : ███████

Date of Action	Seq Nbr	Code	Text
11/22/06	12	WVRAA	Defendant waives reading and advisement of the Original Complaint.
	13	PLNGA	**To the Original Complaint defendant pleads NOT GUILTY to all counts.**
	14	DFDAG	Defendant denies allegations.
	15	CLSET	**Pre Trial set on 01/09/2007 at 08:30 AM in Department H2.**
	16	CLSET	**Preliminary Hearing set on 01/17/2007 at 08:30 AM in Department H2.**
	17	WVTPH	Court finds the defendant understandingly, knowingly, and voluntarily waives the right to a Preliminary Hearing within 10 court days/60 calendar days of arraignment.
	18	PLCJN	Counsel joins in waivers.
	19	MOTBY	Motion by Defense for bail reduction
	20	MOTION	Motion granted.
	21	BLSET	Court orders bail set in the amount of $40, 000.00.
	22	DFREM	Defendant remanded to the custody of the Sheriff.
	23	NTJAL	**Notice to Sheriff issued.**
	24	FIFPC	Fingerprint card is received and filed.
11/30/06	1	FIBND	**Surety Bond # S100-01136444 filed.**
12/01/06	1	BBPST	Bail Bond Number S100-01136444 posted in the amount of $40000.00 by GOLDB of SENEC.
01/09/07	1	HHELD	**Hearing held on 01/09/2007 at 08:30:00 AM in Department H2 for Pre Trial.**
	2	OFJUD	Officiating Judge: Peter J. Polos, Judge
	3	OFJA	Clerk: M. Johnson
	4	OFBAL	Bailiff: L. Martinez
	5	OFREP	Court Reporter: Marcia Gahring
	6	APDDA	People represented by Matthew Zandi, Deputy District Attorney, present.
	7	APNDC	Defendant not present in Court represented by Robert M Brodney, Retained Attorney.
	8	APTXT	Defendant inadvertanly brought to Central Justice Center
	9	WVCRP	Court reporter waived by all parties.

MINUTES

Case : 06HF2202 F A

Name : ▮▮▮▮▮▮▮▮▮▮

Date of Action	Seq Nbr	Code	Text
01/09/07	10	CLCON	Pre Trial continued to 01/12/2007 at 08:30 AM in Department H2 at request of Defense.
	11	BLPBS	Present bail deemed sufficient and continued.
	12	TXKPW	Keep with companion cases(s) 07HF0020, 03SF0869.
01/12/07	1	HHELD	Hearing held on 01/12/2007 at 08:30:00 AM in Department H2 for Pre Trial.
	2	OFJUD	Officiating Judge: Peter J. Polos, Judge
	3	OFJA	Clerk: M. Johnson
	4	OFBAL	Bailiff: J. Winovich
	5	OFREP	Court Reporter: Marcia Gahring
	6	APDDA	People represented by George W. McFetridge Jr., Deputy District Attorney, present.
	7	APDWRA	Defendant present in Court with counsel Brodney, Robert M, Retained Attorney.
	8	CLVAC	Preliminary Hearing vacated for 01/17/2007 at 08:30 AM in H2.
	9	CLCON	Pre Trial continued to 02/15/2007 at 08:30 AM in Department H2 by stipulation of all parties.
	10	WVTIM	Defendant waives statutory time for Preliminary Hearing.
	11	BLPBS	Present bail deemed sufficient and continued.
	12	TXKPW	Keep with companion cases(s) 07HF0020 & 03SF0869.
	13	OFMEC	Minutes entered by R. Hume.
02/15/07	1	HHELD	Hearing held on 02/15/2007 at 08:30:00 AM in Department H2 for Pre Trial.
	2	OFJUD	Officiating Judge: Peter J. Polos, Judge
	3	OFJA	Clerk: T. Hauck
	4	OFBAL	Bailiff: J. Winovich
	5	OFREP	Court Reporter: Marcia Gahring
	6	APDDA	People represented by George W. McFetridge Jr., Deputy District Attorney, present.
	7	APSPC	Susan L. Angell makes a special appearance for Robert M Brodney, Retained Attorney. Defendant present.
	8	CLCON	Pre Trial continued to 03/27/2007 at 08:30 AM in Department H2 at request of Defense.

MINUTES

Case : 06HF2202 F A

Name : ███████████

Date of Action	Seq Nbr	Code	Text
02/15/07	9	WVTPH	Court finds the defendant understandingly, knowingly, and voluntarily waives the right to a Preliminary Hearing within 60 calendar days of arraignment.
	10	PLCJN	Counsel joins in waivers.
	11	DFOTR	Defendant ordered to appear.
	12	BLSTR	Current bail set for defendant to remain.
	13	TXKPW	Keep with companion cases(s) 07HF0020, 03SF0869.
03/27/07	1	HHELD	Hearing held on 03/27/2007 at 08:30:00 AM in Department H2 for Pre Trial.
	2	OFJUD	Officiating Judge: Peter J. Polos, Judge
	3	OFJA	Clerk: K. Reinke
	4	OFBAL	Bailiff: J. Winovich
	5	OFREP	Court Reporter: Marcia Gahring
	6	APDDA	People represented by George W. McFetridge Jr., Deputy District Attorney, present.
	7	APDWRA	Defendant present in Court with counsel Brodney, Robert M, Retained Attorney.
	8	CLSET	Pre Trial set on 05/07/2007 at 08:30 AM in Department H2.
	9	WVTIM	Defendant waives statutory time for Preliminary Hearing.
	10	PLCJN	Counsel joins in waivers.
	11	DFOTR	Defendant ordered to return.
	12	BLSTR	Current bail set for defendant to remain.
	13	DFREM	Defendant remanded to the custody of the Sheriff.
	14	NTJAL	Notice to Sheriff issued.
	15	TXKPW	Keep with companion cases(s) 03SF0869 and 07HF0020.
	16	TEXT	Correction: (Entered NUNC_PRO_TUNC on 04/03/07)
	17	NTRCO	Defendant released on this case only. Release issued. (Entered NUNC_PRO_TUNC on 04/03/07)
	18	NTJAL	Notice to Sheriff issued. (Entered NUNC_PRO_TUNC on 04/03/07)
04/03/07	1	NUNCPT	Nunc Pro Tunc entry(s) made on this date for 03/27/2007.
05/07/07	1	HHELD	Hearing held on 05/07/2007 at 08:30:00 AM in Department H2 for Pre Trial.
	2	OFJUD	Officiating Judge: Peter J. Polos, Judge

MINUTES

Case : 06HF2202 F A

Name : ███████████

Date of Action	Seq Nbr	Code	Text
05/07/07	3	OFJA	Clerk: C. B. Henderson
	4	OFBAL	Bailiff: J. Winovich
	5	OFREP	Court Reporter: Marcia Gahring
	6	APDDA	People represented by George W. McFetridge Jr., Deputy District Attorney, present.
	7	APSPC	Brian Cretney makes a special appearance for Robert M Brodney, Retained Attorney. Defendant present.
	8	FIAMD	**First Amended Complaint filed by Orange County District Attorney.**
	9	CTADD	First Amended Complaint now charges COUNT 20, 529(3) PC, FELONY, date of violation 02/08/2006.
	10	CTADD	First Amended Complaint now charges COUNT 21, 496(a) PC, FELONY, date of violation 02/08/2006.
	11	CTADD	First Amended Complaint now charges COUNT 22, 530.5(a) PC, FELONY, date of violation 01/30/2006.
	12	CTADD	First Amended Complaint now charges COUNT 23, 530.5(a) PC, FELONY, date of violation 02/08/2006.
	13	CTADD	First Amended Complaint now charges COUNT 24, 470(d) PC, FELONY, date of violation 02/07/2006.
	14	CTADD	First Amended Complaint now charges COUNT 25, 496(a) PC, FELONY, date of violation 02/08/2006.
	15	CTADD	First Amended Complaint now charges COUNT 26, 11377(a) HS, FELONY, date of violation 02/08/2006.
	16	CTADD	First Amended Complaint now charges COUNT 27, 496(a) PC, FELONY, date of violation 02/08/2006.
	17	CTADD	First Amended Complaint now charges COUNT 28, 459-460(b) PC, FELONY, date of violation 02/07/2006.
	18	CTADD	First Amended Complaint now charges COUNT 29, 476 PC, FELONY, date of violation 02/07/2006.
	19	CTADD	First Amended Complaint now charges COUNT 30, 459-460(b) PC, FELONY, date of violation 02/06/2006.
	20	CTADD	First Amended Complaint now charges COUNT 31, 476 PC, FELONY, date of violation 02/06/2006.
	21	CTADD	First Amended Complaint now charges COUNT 32, 459-460(b) PC, FELONY, date of violation 02/07/2006.
	22	CTADD	First Amended Complaint now charges COUNT 33, 476 PC, FELONY, date of violation 02/07/2006.

MINUTES

Case : 06HF2202 F A

Name : ███████████

Date of Action	Seq Nbr	Code	Text
05/07/07	23	CTADD	First Amended Complaint now charges COUNT 34, 459-460(b) PC, FELONY, date of violation 02/07/2006.
	24	CTADD	First Amended Complaint now charges COUNT 35, 476 PC, FELONY, date of violation 02/07/2006.
	25	CTADD	First Amended Complaint now charges COUNT 36, 459-460(b) PC, FELONY, date of violation 02/07/2006.
	26	CTADD	First Amended Complaint now charges COUNT 37, 476 PC, FELONY, date of violation 02/07/2006.
	27	CTADD	First Amended Complaint now charges COUNT 38, 459-460(b) PC, FELONY, date of violation 02/06/2006.
	28	CTADD	First Amended Complaint now charges COUNT 39, 476 PC, FELONY, date of violation 02/06/2006.
	29	CTADD	First Amended Complaint now charges COUNT 40, 459-460(b) PC, FELONY, date of violation 02/07/2006.
	30	CTADD	First Amended Complaint now charges COUNT 41, 476 PC, FELONY, date of violation 02/07/2006.
	31	CTADD	First Amended Complaint now charges COUNT 42, 459-460(b) PC, FELONY, date of violation 12/10/2005.
	32	CTADD	First Amended Complaint now charges COUNT 43, 476 PC, FELONY, date of violation 12/10/2005.
	33	CTADD	First Amended Complaint now charges COUNT 44, 459-460(b) PC, FELONY, date of violation 11/21/2005.
	34	CTADD	First Amended Complaint now charges COUNT 45, 476 PC, FELONY, date of violation 11/21/2005.
	35	CTADD	First Amended Complaint now charges COUNT 46, 459-460(b) PC, FELONY, date of violation 12/19/2005.
	36	CTADD	First Amended Complaint now charges COUNT 47, 476 PC, FELONY, date of violation 12/19/2005.
	37	CTADD	First Amended Complaint now charges COUNT 48, 459-460(b) PC, FELONY, date of violation 12/24/2005.
	38	CTADD	First Amended Complaint now charges COUNT 49, 476 PC, FELONY, date of violation 12/24/2005.
	39	CTADD	First Amended Complaint now charges COUNT 50, 459-460(b) PC, FELONY, date of violation 12/11/2005.
	40	CTADD	First Amended Complaint now charges COUNT 51, 476 PC, FELONY, date of violation 12/11/2005.
	41	CTADD	First Amended Complaint now charges COUNT 52, 459-460(b) PC, FELONY, date of violation 02/06/2006.

MINUTES

Case : 06HF2202 F A

Name : ████████████

Date of Action	Seq Nbr	Code	Text
05/07/07	42	CTADD	First Amended Complaint now charges COUNT 53, 476 PC, FELONY, date of violation 02/06/2006.
	43	CTADD	First Amended Complaint now charges COUNT 54, 459-460(b) PC, FELONY, date of violation 01/25/2006.
	44	CTADD	First Amended Complaint now charges COUNT 55, 476 PC, FELONY, date of violation 01/25/2006.
	45	CTADD	First Amended Complaint now charges COUNT 56, 496(a) PC, FELONY, date of violation 02/08/2006.
	46	CTADD	First Amended Complaint now charges COUNT 57, 496(a) PC, FELONY, date of violation 02/08/2006.
	47	CTADD	First Amended Complaint now charges COUNT 58, 496(a) PC, FELONY, date of violation 02/08/2006.
	48	CTADD	First Amended Complaint now charges COUNT 59, 496(a) PC, FELONY, date of violation 02/08/2006.
	49	CTADD	First Amended Complaint now charges COUNT 60, 496(a) PC, FELONY, date of violation 01/30/2006.
	50	CPGTO	Copy of First Amended Complaint given to counsel.
	51	CPACK	Counsel acknowledges receipt of the complaint.
	52	WVRAA	Defendant waives reading and advisement of the First Amended Complaint.
	53	PLNGA	**To the First Amended Complaint defendant pleads NOT GUILTY to all counts.**
	54	MORES	Defense reserves all motions.
	55	CLSET	**Pre Trial set on 05/21/2007 at 08:30 AM in Department H2.**
	56	CLSET	**Preliminary Hearing set on 06/05/2007 at 08:30 AM in Department H2.**
	57	WVTPH	Court finds the defendant understandingly, knowingly, and voluntarily waives the right to a Preliminary Hearing within 10 court days of arraignment.
	58	PLCJN	Counsel joins in waivers.
	59	DFOTR	Defendant ordered to appear.
	60	BLPBS	Present bail deemed sufficient and continued.
	61	TXKPW	Keep with companion cases(s) 07HF0020 and 03SF0869.
05/21/07	1	HHELD	Hearing held on 05/21/2007 at 08:30:00 AM in Department H2 for Pre Trial.
	2	OFJUD	Officiating Judge: Kelly MacEachern, Judge

MINUTES

Case : 06HF2202 F A

Name : ▮▮▮▮▮▮▮

Date of Action	Seq Nbr	Code	Text
05/21/07	3	OFJA	Clerk: C. B. Henderson
	4	OFBAL	Bailiff: J. Winovich
	5	OFREP	Court Reporter: Marcia Gahring
	6	APDDA	People represented by George W. McFetridge Jr., Deputy District Attorney, present.
	7	APSUB	Lloyd Freeberg, Retained Attorney, substituting in as Attorney of Record.
	8	APATR	Robert M Brodney relieved as Counsel of Record.
	9	APDWC	Defendant present in Court with counsel Lloyd Freeberg, Retained Attorney.
	10	CLSET	**Pre Trial set on 06/07/2007 at 08:30 AM in Department H2.**
	11	CLSET	**Preliminary Hearing set on 06/28/2007 at 08:30 AM in Department H2.**
	12	WVTIM	Defendant waives statutory time for Preliminary Hearing.
	13	DFOTR	Defendant ordered to appear.
	14	BLPBS	Present bail deemed sufficient and continued.
	15	TXKPW	Keep with companion cases(s) 03SF0869 and 07HF0020.
05/22/07	1	CLCAN	PH set on 06/05/07 at 08:30 AM in H2 has been cancelled.
06/07/07	1	HHELD	**Hearing held on 06/07/2007 at 08:30:00 AM in Department H2 for Pre Trial.**
	2	OFJUD	Officiating Judge: Peter J. Polos, Judge
	3	OFJA	Clerk: T. Hauck
	4	OFBAL	Bailiff: J. Winovich
	5	OFREP	Court Reporter: Marcia Gahring
	6	APDDA	People represented by George W. McFetridge Jr., Deputy District Attorney, present.
	7	APSPC	Martin Joseph Heneghan makes a special appearance for Lloyd Freeberg, Retained Attorney. Defendant present.
	8	CLPTP	**Pretrial off calendar, Preliminary Hearing set on 06/28/2007 at 08:30 AM in H2 to remain.**
	9	DFOTR	Defendant ordered to appear.
	10	BLPBS	Present bail deemed sufficient and continued.

MINUTES

Case : 06HF2202 F A

Name : ▮▮▮▮▮▮▮▮▮▮

Date of Action	Seq Nbr	Code	Text
06/07/07	11	TXKPW	Keep with companion cases(s) 07HF0020, 03SF0869.
06/28/07	1	HHELD	**Hearing held on 06/28/2007 at 08:30:00 AM in Department H2 for Preliminary Hearing.**
	2	OFJUD	Officiating Judge: Peter J. Polos, Judge
	3	OFJA	Clerk: C. B. Henderson
	4	OFBAL	Bailiff: P. Ada
	5	OFREP	Court Reporter: Marcia Gahring
	6	APDDA	People represented by George W. McFetridge Jr., Deputy District Attorney, present.
	7	APSPC	James Sweeney makes a special appearance for Lloyd Freeberg, Retained Attorney. Defendant present.
	8	CLSET	**Pre Trial set on 08/01/2007 at 08:30 AM in Department H2.**
	9	WVTXT	Defendant waives reasonable time. (Entered NUNC_PRO_TUNC on 07/02/07)
	10	DFOTR	Defendant ordered to appear.
	11	BLPBS	Present bail deemed sufficient and continued.
	12	TXKPW	Keep with companion cases(s) 07HF0020 and 03SF0869.
07/02/07	1	NUNCPT	Nunc Pro Tunc entry(s) made on this date for 06/28/2007.
08/01/07	1	HHELD	**Hearing held on 08/01/2007 at 08:30:00 AM in Department H2 for Pre Trial.**
	2	OFJUD	Officiating Judge: Kelly MacEachern, Judge
	3	OFJA	Clerk: T. Hauck
	4	OFBAL	Bailiff: L. Martinez
	5	OFREP	Court Reporter: Lori Shepherd
	6	APDDA	People represented by George W. McFetridge Jr., Deputy District Attorney, present.
	7	APDWRA	Defendant present in Court with counsel Freeberg, Lloyd, Retained Attorney.
	8	CLSET	**Pre Trial set on 10/04/2007 at 08:30 AM in Department H2.**
	9	PBRPO	Probation Department ordered to prepare a Pre-Plea report to be made available to court and counsel 5 days prior to Sentencing.
	10	DFPPR	Defendant is ordered to pay for probation report as determined by the Probation Department.

MINUTES

Case : 06HF2202 F A

Name : ███████████

Date of Action	Seq Nbr	Code	Text
08/01/07	11	WVTIM	Defendant waives statutory time for Preliminary Hearing.
	12	PLCJN	Counsel joins in waivers.
	13	DFOTR	Defendant ordered to appear.
	14	BLPBS	Present bail deemed sufficient and continued.
	15	TXKPW	Keep with companion cases(s) 07HF0020, 03SF0869.
10/04/07	1	HHELD	Hearing held on 10/04/2007 at 08:30:00 AM in Department H2 for Pre Trial.
	2	OFJUD	Officiating Judge: James Odriozola, Commissioner
	3	OFJA	Clerk: C. Le
	4	OFBAL	Bailiff:. Present
	5	OFREP	Court Reporter: Michelle Lott-Megenhofer
	6	OFMEC	Minutes entered by S. Bartush.
	7	APDDA	People represented by George W. McFetridge Jr., Deputy District Attorney, present.
	8	APDWC	Defendant present in Court with counsel Lloyd Freeberg, Retained Attorney.
	9	CLSET	Pre Trial set on 11/06/2007 at 08:30 AM in Department H2.
	10	WVTIM	Defendant waives statutory time for Preliminary Hearing.
	11	BLPBS	Present bail deemed sufficient and continued.
	12	TXKPW	Keep with companion cases(s) 07HF0020.
	13	FITXT	Pre plea filed.
11/06/07	1	HHELD	Hearing held on 11/06/2007 at 08:30:00 AM in Department H2 for Pre Trial.
	2	OFJUD	Officiating Judge: Gregory W. Jones, Commissioner
	3	OFJA	Clerk: M. Johnson
	4	OFBAL	Bailiff: I. Hamdallah
	5	OFREP	Court Reporter: Karen Puckett
	6	APDDA	People represented by George W. McFetridge Jr., Deputy District Attorney, present.
	7	APDWRA	Defendant present in Court with counsel Freeberg, Lloyd, Retained Attorney.
	8	CLCON	Pre Trial continued to 11/29/2007 at 08:30 AM in Department H2 at request of Defense.

MINUTES

Case : 06HF2202 F A

Name : ███████████████

Date of Action	Seq Nbr	Code	Text
11/06/07	9	WVTPH	Court finds the defendant understandingly, knowingly, and voluntarily waives the right to a Preliminary Hearing within 60 calendar days of arraignment.
	10	PLCJN	Counsel joins in waivers.
	11	DFOTR	Defendant ordered to return.
	12	BLPBS	Present bail deemed sufficient and continued.
11/29/07	1	HHELD	**Hearing held on 11/29/2007 at 08:30:00 AM in Department H2 for Pre Trial.**
	2	OFJUD	Officiating Judge: James Odriozola, Commissioner
	3	OFJA	Clerk: K. Reinke
	4	OFBAL	Bailiff: I. Hamdallah
	5	OFREP	Court Reporter: Roxanne Drake
	6	APDDA	People represented by George W. McFetridge Jr., Deputy District Attorney, present.
	7	APDWRA	Defendant present in Court with counsel Freeberg, Lloyd, Retained Attorney.
	8	CLSET	**Pre Trial set on 12/11/2007 at 08:30 AM in Department H2.**
	9	WVTXT	Defendant waives reasonable time.
	10	PLCJN	Counsel joins in waivers.
	11	BLPBS	Present bail deemed sufficient and continued.
	12	FXRLST	Release status of defendant entered in error. Correct release status should reflect: Released on Bond.
12/11/07	1	HHELD	**Hearing held on 12/11/2007 at 08:30:00 AM in Department H2 for Pre Trial.**
	2	OFJUD	Officiating Judge: Gregory W. Jones, Commissioner
	3	OFJA	Clerk: K. Reinke
	4	OFBAL	Bailiff: B. Cate
	5	OFREP	Court Reporter: Tina O'Rourke
	6	APDDA	People represented by George W. McFetridge Jr., Deputy District Attorney, present.
	7	APSPC	Douglas Myers makes a special appearance for Lloyd Freeberg, Retained Attorney. Defendant present.
	8	DFSTC	All Parties being advised of their right to have this matter heard by a Judge of the court have stipulated that the matter be heard by Commissioner Gregory W. Jones.

MINUTES

Case : 06HF2202 F A

Name : █████████████

Date of Action	Seq Nbr	Code	Text
12/11/07	9	FIDOC	Stipulation for Court Commissioner filed.
	10	ADAWV	Defendant advised of and waives the following:
	11	ADJCT	- The right to a trial by Jury.
	12	ADCXW	- The right to confront and cross-examine witnesses.
	13	WVRSI	- The right against self incrimination.
	14	WVRSP	Defendant waives the right to subpoena and present evidence.
	15	PLWTH	**Defendant's motion to WITHDRAW NOT GUILTY PLEA to count(s) 11, 16, 21, 24, 40, 46, 54 granted.**
	16	PLFWR	Court finds defendant intelligently and voluntarily waives legal and constitutional rights to jury trial, confront and examine witnesses, and to remain silent.
	17	PLGCT	**To the First Amended Complaint defendant pleads GUILTY as to count(s) 11, 16, 21, 24, 40, 46, 54.**
	18	FIWWR	Defendant's written waiver of legal and constitutional rights for guilty plea received and ordered filed.
	19	FITXT	Addendum to the Advisement and Waiver of Rights for a Felony Guilty Plea filed.
	20	FITXT	Letter from Wings program, Memo from District Attorney's office filed.
	21	PLFBA	Court finds factual basis and accepts plea.
	22	ADCZS	Defendant advised of the possible consequences of plea affecting deportation and citizenship.
	23	ADMAX	Defendant advised of maximum possible sentence.
	24	ADCSQ	Defendant advised of consequences of violating probation and parole.
	25	PLCPC	This constitutes a prior conviction.
	26	PLCJN	Counsel joins in waivers, pleas, and admissions.
	27	WVAFS	Defendant waives arraignment for sentencing.
	28	PLRIS	Defendant requests immediate sentencing.
	29	WVPBR	Probation report waived.
	30	SPSP1	**No legal cause why judgment should not be pronounced and defendant having been convicted of 530.5(a) PC as charged in count 11, defendant is sentenced to STATE PRISON for Middle term of 2 Year(s) .**

MINUTES

Case : 06HF2202 F A

Name : ▮▮▮▮▮▮▮▮▮▮

Date of Action	Seq Nbr	Code	Text
12/11/07	31	SPAMD	Defendant has also Pled Guilty to the additional charge of 470b PC in count 16 and is sentenced to STATE PRISON for 1/3 the mid term of 8 Months. Sentence imposed to be served consecutive 1/3 non-violent to count 11.
	32	SPAMD	Defendant has also Pled Guilty to the additional charge of 496(a) PC in count 21 and is sentenced to STATE PRISON for 1/3 the mid term of 8 Months. Sentence imposed to be served consecutive 1/3 non-violent to count 11.
	33	SPAMD	Defendant has also Pled Guilty to the additional charge of 470(d) PC in count 24 and is sentenced to STATE PRISON for 1/3 the mid term of 8 Months. Sentence imposed to be served consecutive 1/3 non-violent to count 11.
	34	SPAMD	Defendant has also Pled Guilty to the additional charge of 459-460(b) PC in count 40 and is sentenced to STATE PRISON for 1/3 the mid term of 8 Months. Sentence imposed to be served consecutive 1/3 non-violent to count 11.
	35	SPAMD	Defendant has also Pled Guilty to the additional charge of 459-460(b) PC in count 46 and is sentenced to STATE PRISON for 1/3 the mid term of 8 Months. Sentence imposed to be served consecutive 1/3 non-violent to count 11.
	36	SPAMD	Defendant has also Pled Guilty to the additional charge of 459-460(b) PC in count 54 and is sentenced to STATE PRISON for 1/3 the mid term of 8 Months. Sentence imposed to be served consecutive 1/3 non-violent to count 11.
	37	PRESS	Execution of State Prison sentence is suspended and defendant is placed on 3 Year(s) FORMAL PROBATION as to count(s) 11, 16, 21, 24, 40, 46, 54 on the following terms and conditions:
	38	PRVNL	Violate no law.
	39	PRJAL	Serve 408 Day(s) Orange County Jail as to count(s) 11, 16, 21, 24, 40, 46, 54.
	40	JLCTS	Credit for time served: 272 actual, 136 conduct, totaling 408 days.

Case : 06HF2202 F A

Name : ███████████

Date of Action	Seq Nbr	Code	Text
12/11/07	41	PRSRF	Pay $200.00 Restitution Fine pursuant to Penal Code 1202.4 or Penal Code 1202.4(b).
	42	SESEC	Pay Security Fee(s) pursuant to Penal Code 1465.8 totaling $140.00.
	43	PRRFS	Pay $200.00 Probation Revocation Restitution Fine pursuant to Penal Code 1202.44. Restitution fine stayed, to become effective only upon final revocation of probation.
	44	PRFEP	All fees payable through the Probation Department.
	45	PRTXT	Court finds restitution has been paid in full in the amount of $29, 395.36
	46	PRDNA	Submit to DNA testing pursuant to Penal Code 296.
	47	PRNUD	Use no unauthorized drugs, narcotics, or controlled substances. Submit to drug or narcotic testing as directed by Probation Officer or Police Officer.
	48	PRSAS	Submit your person and property including any residence, premises, container, or vehicle under your control to search and seizure at any time of the day or night by any law enforcement or probation officer with or without a warrant, and with or without reasonable cause or reasonable suspicion.
	49	PRPSY	Cooperate with Probation Officer in any plan for psychiatric, psychological, alcohol and/or drug treatment, or counseling.
	50	PRPOI	Do not possess any other persons' personal identifying information or personal financial information unless approved in advance by your probation officer.
	51	PRNCC2	Do not have blank checks in your possession, nor write any portion of any checks, nor have checking account, nor use or possess credit cards or open credit accounts unless approved.
	52	PRNWP	Do not own, use, or possess any type of dangerous or deadly weapon including any firearms or ammunition.
	53	DFCPP	Defendant provided a copy of "Prohibited Persons Notice Form and Power of Attorney for Firearms and Disposal" pursuant to Penal Code 12021(d)(2).
	54	PROBY	Obey all laws, orders, rules, and regulations of the Court, Jail, and Probation.
	55	PRDTC	Disclose terms and conditions of probation when asked by any law enforcement or probation officer.

MINUTES

Case : 06HF2202 F A

Name : ▮▮▮▮▮▮▮▮▮▮

Date of Action	Seq Nbr	Code	Text
12/11/07	56	PRCN1	Defendant will complete teh Nancy Clerk rehabilitation program for one year
	57	PRPCD	Pay the costs of probation based on the ability to pay as directed by the Probation Officer.
	58	PRFFD	Defendant is required to complete a new financial disclosure form if money is still owing on a restitution order or fine 120 days before the scheduled release from probation. Defendant is required to file the form with the court at least 90 days before the scheduled release from probation.
	59	CDCDM	Count(s) 1, 2, 3, 4, 5, 6, 7, 8, 9, 10 DISMISSED - Motion of People.
	60	CDCDM	Count(s) 12, 13, 14, 15, 17, 18, 19, 20 DISMISSED - Motion of People.
	61	CDCDM	Count(s) 22, 23, 25, 26, 27, 28, 29, 30 DISMISSED - Motion of People.
	62	CDCDM	Count(s) 31, 32, 33, 34, 35, 36, 37, 38, 39 DISMISSED - Motion of People.
	63	CDCDM	Count(s) 41, 42, 43, 44, 45, 47, 48, 49, 50 DISMISSED - Motion of People.
	64	CDCDM	Count(s) 51, 52, 53, 55, 56, 57, 58, 59, 60 DISMISSED - Motion of People.
	65	PRTXT	Complete 1 year Nancy Clark program
	66	PRATC	Defendant accepts terms and conditions of probation.
	67	BLBXN	Court orders bail bond # S100-01136444 exonerated.
	68	DMDEL	DMV Request Deleted. DMV interface DD1 request deleted - No violations to report
12/15/07	1	DOJABS	DOJ Initial Abstract sent.
03/11/08	1	CLADD	**Case calendared on 03/11/08 at 09:30 AM in H2 for MTN MOP.**
	2	HHELD	**Hearing held on 03/11/2008 at 09:30:00 AM in Department H2 for Motion Modification of Probation.**
	3	OFJUD	Officiating Judge: James Odriozola, Commissioner
	4	OFJA	Clerk: M. Johnson
	5	OFBAL	Bailiff: I. Hamdallah
	6	OFREP	Court Reporter: Marcia Gahring

MINUTES

Case : 06HF2202 F A

Name : ███████████

Date of Action	Seq Nbr	Code	Text
03/11/08	7	APDDA	People represented by Chris Kralick, Deputy District Attorney, present.
	8	APWOC	Defendant present in Court without counsel.
	9	MOTBY	Motion by Defense to complete Southern California Community Recovery Center in lieu of Nancy Clark Program
	10	MOTION	Motion granted.
	11	TEXT	Defendant to complete the Southern California Community Recovery Center Program
	12	FITXT	Memorandum from Probation filed.
	13	FITXT	Correspondence from Southern California Community Recovery Center filed.
	14	PBTCR	All terms and conditions of probation are to remain the same.
04/10/09	1	CLCST2	**Probation Violation re: Arraignment set on 04/13/2009 at 09:00 AM in Department C58.**
	2	DSTUP	Defendant's release status updated to reflect: In Custody.
	3	BLNOB	Court orders bail set at NO BAIL.
	4	FIPVP	Probation Violation Petition dated 04/09/2009 filed.
04/13/09	1	HHELD	**Hearing held on 04/13/2009 at 09:00:00 AM in Department C58 for Probation Violation Arraignment.**
	2	OFNOC	# 5 on calendar.
	3	OFJUD	Officiating Judge: Robert R. Fitzgerald, Judge
	4	OFJA	Clerk: B. Ard
	5	OFBAL	Bailiff: D. Scrip
	6	OFREP	Court Reporter: Caryl Axton
	7	APDDA	People represented by Amy Swanson, Deputy District Attorney, present.
	8	APDWRA	Defendant present in Court with counsel Freeberg, Lloyd, Retained Attorney.
	9	TEXT	This case is an execution of sentence suspended and is being returned to the sentencing Judge. Judge Gregory Jones.
	10	CLSET2	**Probation Violation re: Arraignment set on 05/01/2009 at 09:00 AM in Department H2.**

Name: ███████████

Page 17 of 44

MINUTES / ALL CATEGORIES

Case: 06HF2202 F A

2/19/19 2:08 pm

70 | P a g e

MINUTES

Case : 06HF2202 F A

Name : ████████████

Date of Action	Seq Nbr	Code	Text
04/13/09	11	PBREV	Probation ordered revoked as to count(s) 11, 16, 21, 24, 40, 46, 54.
	12	DFOTR	Defendant ordered to appear.
	13	DFREM	Defendant remanded to the custody of the Sheriff.
	14	BLSTR	Current bail set for defendant to remain.
	15	NTJAL	**Notice to Sheriff issued.**
05/01/09	1	HHELD	**Hearing held on 05/01/2009 at 09:00:00 AM in Department H2 for Probation Violation Arraignment.**
	2	OFJUD	Officiating Judge: Gregory W. Jones, Judge
	3	OFJA	Clerk: K. Reinke
	4	OFBAL	Bailiff: B. Cate
	5	OFREP	Court Reporter: Donna Wagner
	6	APSDA	Erin Rowe made a special appearance for District Attorney Jan Christie.
	7	APDWRA	Defendant present in Court with counsel Freeberg, Lloyd, Retained Attorney.
	8	CLCON2	**Probation Violation re: Arraignment continued to 05/29/2009 at 08:30 AM in Department H2 at request of Defense.**
	9	WVTIM	Defendant waives statutory time for Hearing.
	10	PLCJN	Counsel joins in waivers.
	11	DFOTR	Defendant ordered to return.
	12	BLSTR	Current bail set for defendant to remain.
	13	DFREM	Defendant remanded to the custody of the Sheriff.
	14	NTJAL	**Notice to Sheriff issued.**
	15	TXKPW	Keep with companion cases(s) 07HF0020.
05/29/09	1	HHELD	**Hearing held on 05/29/2009 at 08:30:00 AM in Department H2 for Probation Violation Arraignment.**
	2	OFJUD	Officiating Judge: Karen L. Robinson, Judge
	3	OFJA	Clerk: L. Lesar
	4	OFBAL	Bailiff: C. S. Rozean
	5	OFREP	Court Reporter: Donna Wagner
	6	APTXT	Van C. Ho, certified law clerk, appearing specially on the behalf of George McFettride, District Attorney

MINUTES

Case : 06HF2202 F A

Name : ▮▮▮▮▮▮▮▮

Date of Action	Seq Nbr	Code	Text
05/29/09	7	APDWRA	Defendant present in Court with counsel Freeberg, Lloyd, Retained Attorney.
	8	CLCON2	**Probation Violation re: Arraignment continued to 06/12/2009 at 08:30 AM in Department H2 at request of Defense.**
	9	WVTIM	Defendant waives statutory time for Sentencing.
	10	PLCJN	Counsel joins in waivers.
	11	DFOTR	Defendant ordered to return.
	12	BLSTR	Current bail set for defendant to remain.
	13	DFREM	Defendant remanded to the custody of the Sheriff.
	14	NTJAL	**Notice to Sheriff issued.**
	15	TXKPW	Keep with companion cases(s) 07HF0020.
	16	OFMEC	Minutes entered by K. Reinke.
06/12/09	1	HHELD	**Hearing held on 06/12/2009 at 08:30:00 AM in Department H2 for Probation Violation Arraignment.**
	2	OFJUD	Officiating Judge: Karen L. Robinson, Judge
	3	OFJA	Clerk: L. Lesar
	4	OFBAL	Bailiff: C. S. Rozean
	5	OFREP	Court Reporter: Donna Wagner
	6	APTXT	Van Ha, Law Clerk present under supervision of Erin Rowe, Deputy District Attorney specially appearing for George McFettride, Deputy District Attorney
	7	APSDA	Erin Rowe made a special appearance for District Attorney George W. McFetridge Jr..
	8	CLCON2	**Probation Violation re: Arraignment continued to 06/15/2009 at 08:30 AM in Department H2 by stipulation of all parties.**
	9	WVTIM	Defendant waives statutory time for Hearing.
	10	PLCJN	Counsel joins in waivers.
	11	DFOTR	Defendant ordered to appear.
	12	DFREM	Defendant remanded to the custody of the Sheriff.
	13	BLSTR	Current bail set for defendant to remain.
	14	NTJAL	**Notice to Sheriff issued.**
	15	TXKPW	Keep with companion cases(s) 07HF0020.

MINUTES

Case : 06HF2202 F A

Name :

Date of Action	Seq Nbr	Code	Text
06/15/09	1	HHELD	Hearing held on 06/15/2009 at 08:30:00 AM in Department H2 for Probation Violation Arraignment.
	2	OFJUD	Officiating Judge: Gregory W. Jones, Judge
	3	OFJA	Clerk: C. Le
	4	OFBAL	Bailiff: I. Hamdallah
	5	OFREP	Court Reporter: Starlette Soniega-Armijo
	6	APTXT	Van Ha, Certified Law Clerk, appearing specially on behalf of George McFettride, Deputy District Attorney.
	7	APDWC	Defendant present in Court with counsel Lloyd Freeberg, Retained Attorney.
	8	ADLCR	Defendant advised of legal and constitutional rights.
	9	PBADV	Defendant waives right to probation hearing. Defendant admits violation of probation as to count(s) 11, 16, 21, 24, 40, 46, 54.
	10	FDCVP	Court finds defendant in violation of probation.
	11	WVAFS	Defendant waives arraignment for sentencing.
	12	PLCJN	Counsel joins in waivers.
	13	WVTIM	Defendant waives statutory time for Sentencing.
	14	CLSET	Sentencing set on 08/07/2009 at 08:30 AM in Department H2.
	15	DFOTR	Defendant ordered to appear.
	16	BLSTR	Current bail set for defendant to remain.
	17	DFREM	Defendant remanded to the custody of the Sheriff.
	18	NTJAL	Notice to Sheriff issued.
	19	TXKPW	Keep with companion cases(s) 07HF0020.
	20	PBRPO	Probation Department ordered to prepare a Probation & Sentencing report to be made available to court and counsel 5 days prior to Sentencing.
	21	FITXT	Drug Information from Sav-On Pharmacy filed.
	22	FICOR	Correspondence from Theodore G Williams, M.D filed.
	23	FITXT	Forensic Psychological Evaluations from James Gruver, Ph. D., Licensed Psychologist, Dated 05-23-09, placed in confidential envelope and filed.
08/07/09	1	HHELD	Hearing held on 08/07/2009 at 08:30:00 AM in Department H2 for Sentencing.

SUPERIOR COURT OF THE STATE OF CALIFORNIA,
COUNTY OF ORANGE

MINUTES

Case : 06HF2202 F A

Name : ███████████

Date of Action	Seq Nbr	Code	Text
08/07/09	2	OFJUD	Officiating Judge: Gregory W. Jones, Judge
	3	OFJA	Clerk: L. Trottier
	4	OFBAL	Bailiff: B. Cate
	5	OFREP	Court Reporter: Donna Wagner
	6	OFMEC	Minutes entered by T. Lewis.
	7	APDDA	People represented by Beth Carmichael, Deputy District Attorney, present.
	8	APDWRA	Defendant present in Court with counsel Freeberg, Lloyd, Retained Attorney.
	9	CLCON	**Sentencing continued to 08/21/2009 at 08:30 AM in Department H2 at request of Defense.**
	10	DFOTR	Defendant ordered to return.
	11	WVTIM	Defendant waives statutory time for Hearing.
	12	BLSTR	Current bail set for defendant to remain.
	13	DFREM	Defendant remanded to the custody of the Sheriff.
	14	NTJAL	**Notice to Sheriff issued.**
	15	TXKPW	Keep with companion cases(s) 07HF0020.
08/21/09	1	HHELD	**Hearing held on 08/21/2009 at 08:30:00 AM in Department H2 for Sentencing.**
	2	OFJUD	Officiating Judge: Gregory W. Jones, Judge
	3	OFJA	Clerk: M. Johnson
	4	OFBAL	Bailiff: C. F. Cisneros
	5	OFREP	Court Reporter: Donna Cox
	6	APDDA	People represented by Erin Rowe, Deputy District Attorney, present.
	7	APDWRA	Defendant present in Court with counsel Freeberg, Lloyd, Retained Attorney.
	8	CLCON	**Sentencing continued to 09/25/2009 at 08:30 AM in Department H2 by stipulation of all parties.**
	9	WVTIM	Defendant waives statutory time for Sentencing.
	10	FIDOC	Probation & Sentencing report filed.
	11	PLCJN	Counsel joins in waivers.
	12	BLSTR	Current bail set for defendant to remain.
	13	DFREM	Defendant remanded to the custody of the Sheriff.

MINUTES

Case : 06HF2202 F A

Name : ███████

Date of Action	Seq Nbr	Code	Text
08/21/09	14	NTJAL	Notice to Sheriff issued.
09/25/09	1	HHELD	**Hearing held on 09/25/2009 at 08:30:00 AM in Department H2 for Sentencing.**
	2	OFJUD	Officiating Judge: James Odriozola, Commissioner
	3	OFJA	Clerk: L. K. Mc Donald
	4	OFBAL	Bailiff: B. Lohrman
	5	OFREP	Court Reporter: Donna Cox
	6	APDDA	People represented by George W. McFetridge Jr., Deputy District Attorney, present.
	7	APSPC	Laura Lindley makes a special appearance for Lloyd Freeberg, Retained Attorney. Defendant present.
	8	CLSET2	**Probation Violation re: Sentencing set on 10/16/2009 at 08:30 AM in Department H2.**
	9	WVTIM	Defendant waives statutory time for Sentencing.
	10	PLCJN	Counsel joins in waivers.
	11	DFOTR	Defendant ordered to appear.
	12	BLSTR	Current bail set for defendant to remain at $0.00.
	13	DFREM	Defendant remanded to the custody of the Sheriff.
	14	NTJAL	**Notice to Sheriff issued.**
	15	TXKPW	Keep with companion cases(s) 07HF0020.
10/16/09	1	HHELD	**Hearing held on 10/16/2009 at 08:30:00 AM in Department H2 for Probation Violation Sentencing.**
	2	OFJUD	Officiating Judge: Gregory W. Jones, Judge
	3	OFJA	Clerk: T. Lewis
	4	OFBAL	Bailiff: B. Cate
	5	OFREP	Court Reporter: Donna Cox
	6	APDDA	People represented by George W. McFetridge Jr., Deputy District Attorney, present.
	7	APSPC	Tracee May-Brewster makes a special appearance for Lloyd Freeberg, Retained Attorney. Defendant present.
	8	CLCON2	**Probation Violation re: Sentencing continued to 10/22/2009 at 08:30 AM in Department H2 at request of Defense.**
	9	DFOTR	Defendant ordered to return.
	10	BLSTR	Current bail set for defendant to remain at $0.00.

Name: ███████

Page 22 of 44

MINUTES / ALL CATEGORIES

Case: 06HF2202 F A

2/19/10 2:08 pm

75 | P a g e

MINUTES

Case : 06HF2202 F A

Name : ███████████

Date of Action	Seq Nbr	Code	Text
10/16/09	11	DFREM	Defendant remanded to the custody of the Sheriff.
	12	NTJAL	**Notice to Sheriff issued.**
	13	TXKPW	Keep with companion cases(s) 07HF0020.
10/22/09	1	HHELD	**Hearing held on 10/22/2009 at 08:30:00 AM in Department H2 for Probation Violation Sentencing.**
	2	OFJUD	Officiating Judge: Gregory W. Jones, Judge
	3	OFJA	Clerk: L. Sanchez
	4	OFBAL	Bailiff: C. S. Rozean
	5	OFREP	Court Reporter: Donna Cox
	6	APDDA	People represented by Stefanie Marangi, Deputy District Attorney, present.
	7	APDWRA	Defendant present in Court with counsel Freeberg, Lloyd, Retained Attorney.
	8	CLCON2	**Probation Violation re: Sentencing continued to 11/13/2009 at 08:30 AM in Department H2 by stipulation of all parties.**
	9	WVTIM	Defendant waives statutory time for Probation Violation.
	10	BLSTR	Current bail set for defendant to remain at $0.00.
	11	DFOTR	Defendant ordered to appear.
	12	PLCJN	Counsel joins in waivers.
	13	DFREM	Defendant remanded to the custody of the Sheriff.
	14	NTJAL	**Notice to Sheriff issued.**
11/13/09	1	HHELD	**Hearing held on 11/13/2009 at 08:30:00 AM in Department H2 for Probation Violation Sentencing.**
	2	OFJUD	Officiating Judge: Gregory W. Jones, Judge
	3	OFJA	Clerk: L. Trottier
	4	OFBAL	Bailiff: B. Cate
	5	OFREP	Court Reporter: Donna Cox
	6	APDDA	People represented by George W. McFetridge Jr., Deputy District Attorney, present.
	7	APDWRA	Defendant present in Court with counsel Freeberg, Lloyd, Retained Attorney.
	8	CLCON2	**Probation Violation re: Sentencing continued to 11/24/2009 at 08:30 AM in Department H2 at request of Defense.**

Name: ███████████

Page 23 of 44

MINUTES / ALL CATEGORIES

Case: 06HF2202 F A

2/19/19 2:08 pm

76 | Page

MINUTES

Case : 06HF2202 F A

Name : ██████████

Date of Action	Seq Nbr	Code	Text
11/13/09	9	DFOTR	Defendant ordered to appear.
	10	PLCJN	Counsel joins in waivers.
	11	BLSTR	Current bail set for defendant to remain at $0.00.
	12	DFREM	Defendant remanded to the custody of the Sheriff.
	13	NTJAL	**Notice to Sheriff issued.**
	14	TXKPW	Keep with companion cases(s) 07HF0020.
11/24/09	1	HHELD	**Hearing held on 11/24/2009 at 08:30:00 AM in Department H2 for Probation Violation Sentencing.**
	2	OFJUD	Officiating Judge: Robert Gannon, Judge
	3	OFJA	Clerk: L. Taylor
	4	OFBAL	Bailiff: C. S. Rozean
	5	OFREP	Court Reporter: Donna Cox
	6	APDDA	People represented by Cheryl Gold, Deputy District Attorney, present.
	7	APDWRA	Defendant present in Court with counsel Freeberg, Lloyd, Retained Attorney.
	8	WVTIM	Defendant waives statutory time for Sentencing.
	9	PLRIS	Defendant requests immediate sentencing.
	10	PBRSM	Court orders probation reinstated and modified as to count(s) 11, 16, 21, 24, 40, 46, 54 as follows:
	11	SPPSI	**STATE PRISON sentence previously suspended on 12/11/2007 as to count(s) 11 now IMPOSED.**
	12	SPPSI	**STATE PRISON sentence previously suspended on 12/11/2007 as to count(s) 16 now IMPOSED.**
	13	SPPSI	**STATE PRISON sentence previously suspended on 12/11/2007 as to count(s) 21 now IMPOSED.**
	14	SPPSI	**STATE PRISON sentence previously suspended on 12/11/2007 as to count(s) 24 now IMPOSED.**
	15	SPPSI	**STATE PRISON sentence previously suspended on 12/11/2007 as to count(s) 40 now IMPOSED.**
	16	SPPSI	**STATE PRISON sentence previously suspended on 12/11/2007 as to count(s) 46 now IMPOSED.**
	17	SPPSI	**STATE PRISON sentence previously suspended on 12/11/2007 as to count(s) 54 now IMPOSED.**
	18	SPTTP	Total term to be served in State Prison is 6 Year(s) .

MINUTES

Case : 06HF2202 F A

Name : ███████████

Date of Action	Seq Nbr	Code	Text
11/24/09	19	SVPRSN	COURT ORDERS State Prison sentence VACATED. (Entered NUNC_PRO_TUNC on 07/05/11)
	20	SVPCRE	The Court orders State Prison sentence credit ordered on 12/11/2007 vacated. (Entered NUNC_PRO_TUNC on 07/05/11)
	21	SPSP1	No legal cause why judgment should not be pronounced and defendant having been convicted of 530.5(a) PC as charged in count 11, defendant is sentenced to STATE PRISON for Middle term of 2 Year(s) 0 Months. (Entered NUNC_PRO_TUNC on 07/05/11)
	22	SPAMD	Defendant has also Pled Guilty to the additional charge of 470b PC in count 16 and is sentenced to STATE PRISON for 1/3 the mid term of 0 Year(s) 8 Months. Sentence imposed to be served consecutive 1/3 non-violent to count 11. (Entered NUNC_PRO_TUNC on 07/05/11)
	23	SPAC1	Defendant has also Pled Guilty to the additional charge of 496(a) PC in count 21 and is sentenced to STATE PRISON for Middle term of 2 Year(s) 0 Months. Sentence imposed to be served concurrent to count 11. (Entered NUNC_PRO_TUNC on 07/05/11)
	24	SPAC1	Defendant has also Pled Guilty to the additional charge of 470(d) PC in count 24 and is sentenced to STATE PRISON for Middle term of 2 Year(s) 0 Months. Sentence imposed to be served concurrent to count 11. (Entered NUNC_PRO_TUNC on 07/05/11)
	25	SPAC1	Defendant has also Pled Guilty to the additional charge of 459-460(b) PC in count 40 and is sentenced to STATE PRISON for Middle term of 2 Year(s) 0 Months. Sentence imposed to be served concurrent to count 11. (Entered NUNC_PRO_TUNC on 07/05/11)
	26	SPAC1	Defendant has also Pled Guilty to the additional charge of 459-460(b) PC in count 46 and is sentenced to STATE PRISON for Middle term of 2 Year(s) 0 Months. Sentence imposed to be served concurrent to count 11. (Entered NUNC_PRO_TUNC on 07/05/11)

MINUTES

Case : 06HF2202 F A

Name : ████████████

Date of Action	Seq Nbr	Code	Text
11/24/09	27	SPAC1	Defendant has also Pled Guilty to the additional charge of 459-460(b) PC in count 54 and is sentenced to STATE PRISON for Middle term of 2 Year(s) 0 Months. Sentence imposed to be served concurrent to count 11. (Entered NUNC_PRO_TUNC on 07/05/11)
	28	SPCTS1	Credit for time served: 485 actual, 242 conduct, totaling 727 days pursuant to Penal Code 2933(e)(1). (Entered NUNC_PRO_TUNC on 07/05/11)
	29	SPTXT	defendant is also awarded 367 days credit for the completed treatment program. Total custody credits are 1, 094 days. (Entered NUNC_PRO_TUNC on 07/05/11)
	30	SPTTP	Total term to be served in State Prison is 2 Year(s) 8 Months. (Entered NUNC_PRO_TUNC on 07/05/11)
	31	SPPTS	Defendant's prison term has been served. (Entered NUNC_PRO_TUNC on 07/05/11)
	32	SVPRSN	COURT ORDERS State Prison sentence VACATED. (Entered NUNC_PRO_TUNC on 08/21/12)
	33	SVPCRE	The Court orders State Prison sentence credit ordered on 11/24/2009 vacated. (Entered NUNC_PRO_TUNC on 08/21/12)
	34	SPSP1	No legal cause why judgment should not be pronounced and defendant having been convicted of 530.5(a) PC as charged in count 11, defendant is sentenced to STATE PRISON for Middle term of 2 Year(s) 0 Months. (Entered NUNC_PRO_TUNC on 08/21/12)
	35	SPAMD	Defendant has also Pled Guilty to the additional charge of 470b PC in count 16 and is sentenced to STATE PRISON for 1/3 the mid term of 0 Year(s) 8 Months. Sentence imposed to be served consecutive 1/3 non-violent to count 11. (Entered NUNC_PRO_TUNC on 08/21/12)
	36	SPAC1	Defendant has also Pled Guilty to the additional charge of 496(a) PC in count 21 and is sentenced to STATE PRISON for Low term of 1 Year(s) 4 Months. Sentence imposed to be served concurrent to count 11. (Entered NUNC_PRO_TUNC on 08/21/12)

MINUTES

Case : 06HF2202 F A

Name : ████████████

Date of Action	Seq Nbr	Code	Text
11/24/09	37	SPAC1	Defendant has also Pled Guilty to the additional charge of 470(d) PC in count 24 and is sentenced to STATE PRISON for Low term of 1 Year(s) 4 Months. Sentence imposed to be served concurrent to count 11. (Entered NUNC_PRO_TUNC on 08/21/12)
	38	SPAC1	Defendant has also Pled Guilty to the additional charge of 459-460(b) PC in count 40 and is sentenced to STATE PRISON for Low term of 1 Year(s) 4 Months. Sentence imposed to be served concurrent to count 11. (Entered NUNC_PRO_TUNC on 08/21/12)
	39	SPAC1	Defendant has also Pled Guilty to the additional charge of 459-460(b) PC in count 46 and is sentenced to STATE PRISON for Low term of 1 Year(s) 4 Months. Sentence imposed to be served concurrent to count 11. (Entered NUNC_PRO_TUNC on 08/21/12)
	40	SPAC1	Defendant has also Pled Guilty to the additional charge of 459-460(b) PC in count 54 and is sentenced to STATE PRISON for Low term of 1 Year(s) 4 Months. Sentence imposed to be served concurrent to count 11. (Entered NUNC_PRO_TUNC on 08/21/12)
	41	SPCTS1	Credit for time served: 485 actual, 242 conduct, totaling 727 days pursuant to Penal Code 2933(e)(1). (Entered NUNC_PRO_TUNC on 08/21/12)
	42	SPTXT	Defendant is also awarded 367 days credit for the treatment program completed, for total custody credits of 1, 094 days (Entered NUNC_PRO_TUNC on 08/21/12)
	43	SPTTP	Total term to be served in State Prison is 2 Year(s) 8 Months. (Entered NUNC_PRO_TUNC on 08/21/12)
	44	SPPTS	Defendant's prison term has been served. (Entered NUNC_PRO_TUNC on 08/21/12)
	45	PRJLT	Court awards custody credits as follows: 485 days Actual time 242 days Good Time Work Time 367 days program credit Totaling 1, 094 days
	46	PRJLT	Court deems 6 year State Prison Sentence Served
	47	SEDNA	Defendant to submit to DNA testing pursuant to Penal Code 296.

Name: ████████████

Page 27 of 44

MINUTES / ALL CATEGORIES

Case: 06HF2202 F A

2/19/19 2:08 pm

80 | P a g e

MINUTES

Case : 06HF2202 F A

Name : ██████████████

Date of Action	Seq Nbr	Code	Text
11/24/09	48	DFCPP	Defendant provided a copy of "Prohibited Persons Notice Form and Power of Attorney for Firearms and Disposal" pursuant to Penal Code 12021(d)(2).
	49	SESRF	Pay $200.00 Restitution Fine pursuant to Penal Code 1202.4 or Penal Code 1202.4(b).
	50	SPRFS	Pay $200.00 Parole Revocation Restitution Fine pursuant to Penal Code 1202.45. Parole Revocation Restitution Fine suspended unless parole is revoked.
	51	SESEC	Pay $30.00 Security Fee per convicted count pursuant to Penal Code 1465.8.
	52	SECCA	Pay Criminal Conviction Assessment Fee per convicted count of $30.00 per misdemeanor/felony and $35.00 per infraction pursuant to Government Code 70373(a)(1).
	53	SPFDC	Court orders all fees payable through the Department of Corrections.
	54	NTRCO	Defendant released on this case only. Release issued.
	55	NTJAL	**Notice to Sheriff issued.**
	56	DFRPT2	Defendant ordered to report to Department of Corrections Parole Department located at: 1600 No. Main St. Santa Ana, Ca 92702 within 72 hours of release.
	57	PBTRM	Court orders probation terminated as to count(s) 11, 16, 21, 24, 40, 46, 54.
	58	NTJAL	**Notice to Sheriff issued.**
11/25/09	1	NTRCO	Defendant released on this case only. Release issued.
	2	NTJAL	**Notice to Sheriff issued.**
11/29/09	1	DOJABS	DOJ Subsequent Abstract sent.
	2	DOJABS	DOJ Subsequent Abstract sent.
	3	CSCLS	**Case closed.**
12/01/09	1	FISPAJ	Original State Prison Abstract of Judgment - Prison Commitment, Determinate document filed and conformed copy mailed to California Department of Corrections and Rehabilitation, Division of Adult Institutions; Legal Processing Unit.
01/12/11	1	HHELD	**Hearing held on 01/12/2011 at 09:00 AM in Department H5 for Hearing.**
	2	OFJUD	Judicial Officer: Robert Gannon, Judge

MINUTES

Case : 06HF2202 F A

Name : ▮▮▮▮▮▮▮▮▮▮

Date of Action	Seq Nbr	Code	Text
01/12/11	3	OFJA	Clerk: L. Fields
	4	OFBAL	Bailiff:. Present
	5	OFREP	Court Reporter: Karen Puckett
	6	APDDA	People represented by Nikki Chambers, Deputy District Attorney, present.
	7	APNDC	Defendant not present in Court represented by Lloyd Freeberg, Retained Attorney.
	8	CLCON	Hearing continued to 02/02/2011 at 08:30 AM in Department H5 by stipulation of all parties.
	9	CLTXT	To address the State Prison Credits
	10	DFOTR	Defendant ordered to appear.
02/02/11	1	HHELD	Hearing held on 02/02/2011 at 08:30:00 AM in Department H5 for Hearing.
	2	OFJUD	Judicial Officer: Robert Gannon, Judge
	3	OFJA	Clerk: L. Fields
	4	OFBAL	Bailiff: A. M. Fletcher
	5	OFREP	Court Reporter: None
	6	APTXT	Appearance made by George W. McFetridge, Deputy District Attorney, by telephone
	7	APSPC	Laura Lindley makes a special appearance for Lloyd Freeberg, Retained Attorney. Defendant present.
	8	FDTXT	Court finds good cause for a continuance due to illness of defense counsel
	9	CLCON	Hearing continued to 03/03/2011 at 08:30 AM in Department H5 at request of Defense.
	10	DFOTR	Defendant ordered to appear.
03/03/11	1	HHELD	Hearing held on 03/03/2011 at 08:30:00 AM in Department H5 for Hearing.
	2	OFJUD	Judicial Officer: Robert Gannon, Judge
	3	OFJA	Clerk: L. Fields
	4	OFBAL	Bailiff: A. M. Fletcher
	5	OFREP	Court Reporter: None
	6	APNDA	District Attorney not present in Court.
	7	APDWRA	Defendant present in Court with counsel Freeberg, Lloyd, Retained Attorney.

MINUTES

Case : 06HF2202 F A

Name : ██████████

Date of Action	Seq Nbr	Code	Text
03/03/11	8	CLCON	Hearing continued to 03/28/2011 at 08:30 AM in Department H5 at request of Defense.
	9	DFOTR	Defendant ordered to appear.
	10	DSROR	Court orders defendant released on own recognizance.
	11	FISOR	Agreement for Release on Own Recognizance signed and filed.
03/28/11	1	HHELD	Hearing held on 03/28/2011 at 08:30:00 AM in Department H5 for Hearing.
	2	OFJUD	Judicial Officer: Robert Gannon, Judge
	3	OFJA	Clerk: L. Fields
	4	OFBAL	Bailiff: A. M. Fletcher
	5	OFREP	Court Reporter: None
	6	APDDA	People represented by Pete Pierce, Deputy District Attorney, present.
	7	APTXT	Appearance made by Pete Pierce, Deputy District Attorney, by telephone
	8	APSPC	Sheri R Sandecki makes a special appearance for Lloyd Freeberg, Retained Attorney. Defendant present.
	9	CLCON	Hearing continued to 04/07/2011 at 08:30 AM in Department H5 at request of Defense.
	10	WVTIM	Defendant waives statutory time for Hearing.
	11	PLCJN	Counsel joins in waivers.
	12	DFOTR	Defendant ordered to appear.
	13	DSOCN	Defendant's release on own recognizance continued.
04/06/11	1	CLTRAN	Calendar Line for HRG transferred from H5 on 04/07/2011 at 08:30 AM to H2 on 04/07/2011 at 08:30 AM.
04/07/11	1	HHELD	Hearing held on 04/07/2011 at 08:30:00 AM in Department H2 for Hearing.
	2	OFJUD	Judicial Officer: Robert Gannon, Judge
	3	OFJA	Clerk: L. Fields
	4	OFBAL	Bailiff:. Present
	5	OFREP	Court Reporter: Donna Cox
	6	APNDA	District Attorney not present in Court.

MINUTES

Case : 06HF2202 F A

Name : ███████████

Date of Action	Seq Nbr	Code	Text
04/07/11	7	APDWRA	Defendant present in Court with counsel Freeberg, Lloyd, Retained Attorney.
	8	CLCON	**Hearing continued to 05/17/2011 at 08:30 AM in Department H5 at request of Defense.**
	9	DFOTR	Defendant ordered to appear.
	10	DSOCN	Defendant's release on own recognizance continued.
	11	FISOR	Agreement for Release on Own Recognizance signed and filed.
05/17/11	1	HHELD	**Hearing held on 05/17/2011 at 08:30:00 AM in Department H5 for Hearing.**
	2	OFJUD	Judicial Officer: Robert Gannon, Judge
	3	OFJA	Clerk: L. Fields
	4	OFBAL	Bailiff: A. M. Fletcher
	5	OFREP	Court Reporter: Kristy Damron
	6	APSDA	Nikki Chambers made a special appearance for District Attorney George William McFetridge Jr.
	7	APDWRA	Defendant present in Court with counsel Freeberg, Lloyd, Retained Attorney.
	8	CLCON	**Hearing continued to 05/31/2011 at 09:00 AM in Department H5 at request of Defense.**
	9	DFOTR	Defendant ordered to appear.
	10	DSOCN	Defendant's release on own recognizance continued.
	11	FISOR	Agreement for Release on Own Recognizance signed and filed.
05/31/11	1	HHELD	**Hearing held on 05/31/2011 at 09:00:00 AM in Department H5 for Hearing.**
	2	OFJUD	Judicial Officer: Robert Gannon, Judge
	3	OFJA	Clerk: L. Fields
	4	OFBAL	Bailiff: A. M. Fletcher
	5	OFREP	Court Reporter: Karen Puckett
	6	APDDA	People represented by George William McFetridge Jr, Deputy District Attorney, present.
	7	APDWRA	Defendant present in Court with counsel Freeberg, Lloyd, Retained Attorney.
	8	CLCON	**Hearing continued to 06/03/2011 at 08:30 AM in Department H5 at request of Defense.**

MINUTES

Case : 06HF2202 F A

Name : ███████████

Date of Action	Seq Nbr	Code	Text
05/31/11	9	DFOTR	Defendant ordered to appear.
	10	DSOCN	Defendant's release on own recognizance continued.
06/03/11	1	HHELD	**Hearing held on 06/03/2011 at 08:30:00 AM in Department H5 for Hearing.**
	2	OFJUD	Judicial Officer: Robert Gannon, Judge
	3	OFJA	Clerk: L. Fields
	4	OFBAL	Bailiff: A. M. Fletcher
	5	OFREP	Court Reporter: Marcia Gahring
	6	APDDA	People represented by George William McFetridge Jr, Deputy District Attorney, present.
	7	APDWRA	Defendant present in Court with counsel Freeberg, Lloyd, Retained Attorney.
	8	FITXT	Stipulation re: defendant's state prison credits filed.
	9	TEXT	District Attorney and defense counsel stipulate to withdraw the previously filed stipulation
	10	CLCON	**Hearing continued to 06/14/2011 at 09:00 AM in Department H5 by stipulation of all parties.**
	11	DFOTR	Defendant ordered to appear.
	12	DSOCN	Defendant's release on own recognizance continued.
06/14/11	1	HHELD	**Hearing held on 06/14/2011 at 09:00:00 AM in Department H5 for Hearing.**
	2	OFJUD	Judicial Officer: Robert Gannon, Judge
	3	OFJA	Clerk: L. Fields
	4	OFBAL	Bailiff: A. M. Fletcher
	5	OFREP	Court Reporter: Marcia Gahring
	6	APDDA	People represented by George William McFetridge Jr, Deputy District Attorney, present.
	7	APDWRA	Defendant present in Court with counsel Freeberg, Lloyd, Retained Attorney.
	8	CLCON	**Hearing continued to 06/29/2011 at 09:00 AM in Department H5 by stipulation of all parties.**
	9	DFOTR	Defendant ordered to appear.
	10	DSOCN	Defendant's release on own recognizance continued.
	11	FISOR	Agreement for Release on Own Recognizance signed and filed.

Name: ███████████

Page 32 of 44

MINUTES / ALL CATEGORIES

Case: 06HF2202 F A

2/19/19 2:08 pm

85 | P a g e

MINUTES

Case : 06HF2202 F A

Name : ▮▮▮▮▮▮▮▮

Date of Action	Seq Nbr	Code	Text
06/17/11	1	HHELD	Hearing held on 06/17/2011 at 04:00 PM in Department H5 for Chambers Work.
	2	OFJUD	Judicial Officer: Robert Gannon, Judge
	3	OFJA	Clerk: L. Fields
	4	OFBAL	Bailiff:. Present
	5	OFREP	Court Reporter: None
	6	APNDA	District Attorney not present in Court.
	7	APDNC	Defendant not present in court.

Case : 06HF2202 F A

Name : ███████████

Date of Action	Seq Nbr	Code	Text
06/17/11	8	TEXT	In a first amended complaint filed on May 7, 2007, defendant was charged with 59 felony counts and 1 misdemeanor count. Pursuant to a plea agreement negotiated with the District Attorney, on December 11, 2007 defendant entered guilty pleas to 7 felony counts, and was sentenced to a total of 6 years in state prison, with a 2 year sentence on count 11, and terms of 8 months consecutive on each of 6 additional felony counts (counts 16, 21, 24, 40, 46, and 54). Execution of sentence was suspended, defendant was placed on 3 years formal probation on conditions which included serving 408 days in the Orange County jail, and completion of the one-year Nancy Clark treatment program. Defendant was given credit for 272 actual days served and 136 conduct for a total credit of 408 days.

On April 9, 2009, a Probation Violation petition was filed, and probation was revoked on April 13, 2009. On June 15, 2009, defendant was found in violation of probation. Sentencing was continued several times at defendant?s request with the concurrence of the District Attorney. On November 24, 2009, defendant was sentenced to a total of 6 years in state prison, with total credits of 1094 days.

At the time of sentencing on November 24, 2009, it was represented to the sentencing court that the parties had agreed, with the concurrence of a different judge who had found defendant in violation of probation, that defendant should serve in custody a term corresponding to a term with total credits of 1094 days, which the parties then believed also corresponded to the sentence of 6 years. Relying on this representation, the sentencing court sentenced defendant to a term of 6 years, awarded credits of 1094 days, and deemed the 6 year sentence to have been served.

A letter dated December 17, 2010 from the Department of Corrections and Rehabilitation was sent to the court. The letter advised that the awarding of 1094 days credit did not correspond to a 6 year sentence, and that, given the then applicable formula for calculating credits, 2191 days credit would be the correct amount of credited time corresponding to a sentence of 6 years.

It is now apparent that the previously agreed upon calculation that total credits of 1094 days corresponded to a 6 year sentence was in error.

Under Penal Code, section 1170 subdivision (d), a trial court at any time upon the recommendation of the Director of Corrections, may recall a sentence and

Name: ███████████

Page 34 of 44

MINUTES / ALL CATEGORIES

Case: 06HF2202 F A

2/19/19 2:08 pm

87 | P a g e

Case : 06HF2202 F A

Name :

Date of Action	Seq Nbr	Code	Text

commitment and ?resentence the defendant in the same manner as if he or she had not previously been sentenced, provided the new sentence, if any, is no greater than the initial sentence.? People v. Hill, 185 Cal.App.3d 831, 834 (1986).

As to the terms of imprisonment only, the court hereby re-sentences defendant, nunc pro tunc, to a term of two years on count 11, and 8 months consecutive on count 16, and 8 months concurrent on each of the following counts: counts 21, 24, 40, 46, and 54, for a total term of imprisonment of 2 years, 8 months. Defendant is awarded credits of 485 days actual custody time with 242 days conduct credits, and 367 days credit for the treatment program defendant completed, for total credits of 1094 days. Defendant is deemed to have served the custody sentence imposed in this re-sentencing.

The clerk is directed to prepare an Amended Abstract of Judgment reflecting the terms of the re-sentencing, and to forward a copy of same to the Department of Corrections and Rehabilitation.

The clerk is also directed to give written notice of this ruling to the parties.

	9 CLTRM	**Hearing for 06/29/2011 09:00 AM in H5 to remain.**
	10 TEXT	Minute Order sent to Deputy District Attorney and Defense Counsel.
06/29/11	1 HHELD	**Hearing held on 06/29/2011 at 09:00:00 AM in Department H5 for Hearing.**
	2 OFJUD	Judicial Officer: Robert Gannon, Judge
	3 OFJA	Clerk: L. Fields
	4 OFBAL	Bailiff:. Present
	5 OFREP	Court Reporter: None
	6 APDDA	People represented by George William McFetridge Jr, Deputy District Attorney, present.
	7 APDWRA	Defendant present in Court with counsel Freeberg, Lloyd, Retained Attorney.
	8 TEXT	Court orders minutes of 11/24/09 nun pro tunc'd to reflect amended state prison sentence
	9 TEXT	Court orders an amended state prison abstract be prepared

MINUTES

Case : 06HF2202 F A

Name :

Date of Action	Seq Nbr	Code	Text
07/05/11	1	NUNCPT	Nunc Pro Tunc entry(s) made on this date for 11/24/2009.
	46	NUNCPT	Nunc Pro Tunc entry(s) made on this date for 11/24/2009 12:00:00 AM.
09/20/11	1	FISPAJ	Amended State Prison Abstract of Judgment - Prison Commitment, Determinate document filed and conformed copy mailed to California Department of Corrections and Rehabilitation, Division of Adult Institutions; Legal Processing Unit.
10/18/11	1	TXFWD	Letter from the Department of Corrections and Rehabilitation - Division of Adult Institutuions forwarded to Harbor Justice Center - Newport Beach Facility from Central Justice Center.
10/20/11	1	TXRFR	Case referred to Department H5 for review.
10/26/11	1	HHELD	Hearing held on 10/26/2011 at 09:00 AM in Department H5 for Chambers Work.
	2	OFJUD	Judicial Officer: Robert Gannon, Judge
	3	OFJA	Clerk: L. Fields
	4	OFBAL	Bailiff:. Present
	5	OFREP	Court Reporter: None
	6	APNDA	District Attorney not present in Court.
	7	APDNC	Defendant not present in court.
	8	CORAC	Court read and considered Letter from Department of Corrections and Rahabilitation dated 9/29/11.
	9	TEXT	Response letter sent to Linda Ledford at Department of Corrections and Rahabilitation via fax and mail, awaiting clarification of discrepancy
03/09/12	1	HHELD	Hearing held on 03/09/2012 at 08:30 AM in Department H5 for Hearing.
	2	OFJUD	Judicial Officer: Robert Gannon, Judge
	3	OFJA	Clerk: L. Fields
	4	OFBAL	Bailiff: R. T. Cruz
	5	OFREP	Court Reporter: None
	6	APDDA	People represented by George William McFetridge Jr, Deputy District Attorney, present.
	7	APDWRA	Defendant present in Court with counsel Freeberg, Lloyd, Retained Attorney.

MINUTES

Case : 06HF2202 F A

Name : ███████████

Date of Action	Seq Nbr	Code	Text
03/09/12	8	CLCON	Hearing continued to 04/13/2012 at 01:30 PM in Department H5 by stipulation of all parties.
	9	CLTXT	Re: Writ to be filed or stipulated sentence modification/ correction
	10	NTRMO	Electronic Minute Order sent to the Probation Department.
04/13/12	1	HHELD	Hearing held on 04/13/2012 at 01:30:00 PM in Department H5 for Hearing.
	2	OFJUD	Judicial Officer: Robert Gannon, Judge
	3	OFJA	Clerk: L. Fields
	4	OFBAL	Bailiff: C. H. Joyce
	5	OFREP	Court Reporter: None
	6	APTXT	Appearance made by George McFetridge, Deputy District Attorney by telephone.
	7	APTEL	Appearance made by Lloyd Freeberg Retained Attorney by telephone.
	8	TEXT	Due to illness of defense counsel
	9	CLCON	Hearing continued to 05/01/2012 at 01:30 PM in Department H5 by stipulation of all parties.
05/01/12	1	HHELD	Hearing held on 05/01/2012 at 01:30:00 PM in Department H5 for Hearing.
	2	OFJUD	Judicial Officer: Robert Gannon, Judge
	3	OFJA	Clerk: L. Fields
	4	OFBAL	Bailiff: R. O. Coleman
	5	OFREP	Court Reporter: None
	6	APTXT	Appearance made by George William McFetridge Deputy District Attorney by telephone.
	7	APTEL	Appearance made by Lloyd Freeberg Retained Attorney by telephone.
	8	CLCON	Hearing continued to 06/01/2012 at 01:30 PM in Department H5 by stipulation of all parties.
06/01/12	1	HHELD	Hearing held on 06/01/2012 at 01:30:00 PM in Department H5 for Hearing.
	2	OFJUD	Judicial Officer: Robert Gannon, Judge
	3	OFJA	Clerk: L. Fields
	4	OFBAL	Bailiff: J. Ellison

MINUTES

Case : 06HF2202 F A

Name : █████████

Date of Action	Seq Nbr	Code	Text
06/01/12	5	OFREP	Court Reporter: None
	6	APDDA	People represented by George William McFetridge Jr, Deputy District Attorney, present.
	7	APWOC	Defendant present in Court without counsel.
	8	TRIOC	In open court at 01:58 PM
	9	TEXT	Court notes no contact by defense counsel
	10	CLSET	**Sentencing set on 06/07/2012 at 02:00 PM in Department H5.**
	11	DFOTR	Defendant ordered to appear.
06/07/12	1	HHELD	**Hearing held on 06/07/2012 at 02:00:00 PM in Department H5 for Sentencing.**
	2	OFJUD	Judicial Officer: Robert Gannon, Judge
	3	OFJA	Clerk: L. Fields
	4	OFBAL	Bailiff: J. A. Monroe
	5	OFREP	Court Reporter: Kristy Damron
	6	APDDA	People represented by George William McFetridge Jr, Deputy District Attorney, present.
	7	APDWRA	Defendant present in Court with counsel Freeberg, Lloyd, Retained Attorney.
	8	TRIOC	In open court at 02:13 PM

Name: █████████

Page 38 of 44

MINUTES / ALL CATEGORIES

Case: 06HF2202 F A

2/19/19 2:08 pm

91 | P a g e

MINUTES

Case : 06HF2202 F A

Name : ███████████

Date of Action	Seq Nbr	Code	Text
06/07/12	9	TEXT	In a first amended complaint filed on May 7, 2007, defendant was charged with 59 felony counts and 1 misdemeanor count. Pursuant to a plea agreement negotiated with the District Attorney, on December 11, 2007 defendant entered guilty pleas to 7 felony counts, and was sentenced to a total of 6 years in state prison, with a 2 year sentence on count 11, and terms of 8 months consecutive on each of 6 additional felony counts (counts 16, 21, 24, 40, 46, and 54). Execution of sentence was suspended, defendant was placed on 3 years formal probation on conditions which included serving 408 days in the Orange County jail, and completion of the one-year Nancy Clark treatment program. Defendant was given credit for 272 actual days served and 136 conduct for a total credit of 408 days.

On April 9, 2009, a Probation Violation petition was filed, and probation was revoked on April 13, 2009. On June 15, 2009, defendant was found in violation of probation. Sentencing was continued several times at defendant?s request with the concurrence of the District Attorney. On November 24, 2009, defendant was sentenced to a total of 6 years in state prison, with total credits of 1094 days. At the time of sentencing on November 24, 2009, it was represented to the sentencing court that the parties had agreed, with the concurrence of a different judge who had found defendant in violation of probation, that defendant should serve in custody a term corresponding to a term with total credits of 1094 days, which the parties then believed also corresponded to the sentence of 6 years. Relying on this representation, the sentencing court sentenced defendant to a term of 6 years, awarded credits of 1094 days, and deemed the 6 year sentence to have been served.

A letter dated December 17, 2010 from the Department of Corrections and Rehabilitation was sent to the court. The letter advised that the awarding of 1094 days credit did not correspond to a 6 year sentence, and that, given the then applicable formula for calculating credits, 2191 days credit would be the correct amount of credited time corresponding to a sentence of 6 years.

It is now apparent that the previously agreed upon calculation that total credits of 1094 days corresponded to a 6 year sentence was in error.

Under Penal Code, section 1170 subdivision (d), a trial court at any time upon the recommendation of the Director of Corrections, may recall a sentence and

Case : 06HF2202 F A

Name : ▆▆▆▆▆▆▆▆▆▆▆

Date of Action	Seq Nbr	Code	Text
			commitment and resentence the defendant in the same manner as if he or she had not previously been sentenced, provided the new sentence, if any, is no greater than the initial sentence. People v. Hill, 185 Cal.App.3d 831, 834 (1986). As to the terms of imprisonment only, the court hereby re-sentences defendant, nunc pro tunc, to a term of two years on count 11, and 8 months consecutive on count 16, and 16 months concurrent on each of the following counts: counts 21, 24, 40, 46, and 54, for a total term of imprisonment of 2 years, 8 months. Defendant is awarded credits of 485 days actual custody time with 242 days conduct credits, and 367 days credit for the treatment program defendant completed, for total credits of 1094 days. Defendant is deemed to have served the custody sentence imposed in this re-sentencing.
	10 TEXT		Court orders and Amended Abstract of Judgment reflecting the terms of the re-sentencing, and to forward a copy of the same to the Department of Corrections and Rehabilitation
08/21/12	1 NUNCPT		Nunc Pro Tunc entry(s) made on this date for 11/24/2009.
08/22/12	1 FISPAJ		Amended Felony Abstract of Judgment State Prison Commitment, Determinate document filed and conformed copy mailed to California Department of Corrections and Rehabilitation, Division of Adult Institutions; Legal Processing Unit.
05/22/18	1 SEFEE		Pay FEE of $150.00 Change of Plea Fee pursuant to Penal Code 1203.4, 1203.41 & 1203.42.
	2 REMRC		Remittance from receipt # 16248022 received in the amount of $ 150.00.
	3 FIMTN		Defense Motion to Dismiss (PC1203.4) filed.
	4 FITXT		petiton for relief under penal code 1203.4, 1203.4a, 1203.41, 1203.42 filed.
	5 FIDOC		Proof of Service filed.
	6 CLCST2		**Motion re: Dismiss [Penal Code 1203.4/1203.4a/1203.41] set on 07/06/2018 at 08:30 AM in Department C53.**
07/06/18	1 HHELD		Hearing held on 07/06/2018 at 08:30:00 AM in Department C53 for Motion Dismiss [Penal Code 1203.4/1203.4a/1203.41/1203.42].
	2 OFJUD		Judicial Officer: Gary M Pohlson, Judge

MINUTES

Case : 06HF2202 F A

Name : ███████████

Date of Action	Seq Nbr	Code	Text
07/06/18	3	OFJA	Clerk: A. Garcia
	4	OFBAL	Bailiff: J. L. Mc Million
	5	OFREP	Court Reporter: Kimberly R Moore
	6	APDAW	District Attorney waives appearance.
	7	APDWRA	Defendant present in Court with counsel Saif Rahman, Retained Attorney.
	8	MOTBY	Oral motion by Defense for the motion to be continued, heard.
	9	MOTION	Motion granted.
	10	CLCON2	Motion re: Dismiss [Penal Code 1203.4/1203.4a/1203.41/1203.42] continued to 07/20/2018 at 08:30 AM in Department C53 at request of Defense.
07/20/18	1	HHELD	Hearing held on 07/20/2018 at 08:30:00 AM in Department C53 for Motion Dismiss [Penal Code 1203.4/1203.4a/1203.41/1203.42].
	2	OFJUD	Judicial Officer: Gary M Pohlson, Judge
	3	OFJA	Clerk: N. Robles
	4	OFBAL	Bailiff: E. F. Richardson
	5	OFREP	Court Reporter: Andrea Gaunt
	6	APDDA	People represented by George William McFetridge Jr, Deputy District Attorney, present.
	7	APDWRA	Defendant present in Court with counsel Saif Rahman, Retained Attorney.
	8	CLCON2	Motion re: Dismiss [Penal Code 1203.4/1203.4a/1203.41/1203.42] continued to 09/14/2018 at 09:00 AM in Department C49 by stipulation of all parties.
	9	FXCEN2	Motion re: Dismiss [Penal Code 1203.4/1203.4a/1203.41/1203.42] on 09/14/2018 at 09:00 AM in C49 entered in error. (Entered NUNC_PRO_TUNC on 08/30/18)
	10	CLCON2	Motion re: Dismiss [Penal Code 1203.4/1203.4a/1203.41/1203.42] continued to 09/14/2018 at 08:30 AM in Department C53 by stipulation of all parties. (Entered NUNC_PRO_TUNC on 08/30/18)

MINUTES

Case : 06HF2202 F A

Name : ▓▓▓▓▓▓▓▓

Date of Action	Seq Nbr	Code	Text
07/20/18	11	OFMCD	Minutes entered by E. Villela on 07/20/2018.
08/30/18	1	NUNCPT	Nunc Pro Tunc entry(s) made on this date for 07/20/2018.
09/14/18	1	HHELD	**Hearing held on 09/14/2018 at 08:30:00 AM in Department C53 for Motion Dismiss [Penal Code 1203.4/1203.4a/1203.41/1203.42].**
	2	OFJUD	Judicial Officer: Gary M Pohlson, Judge
	3	OFJA	Clerk: N. Robles
	4	OFBAL	Bailiff: E. F. Richardson
	5	OFREP	Court Reporter: Wendy Tatreau
	6	APSDA	Susan Lee made a special appearance for District Attorney George William McFetridge Jr.
	7	APNDC	Defendant not present in Court represented by Saif Rahman, Retained Attorney.
	8	CLCON2	**Motion re: Dismiss [Penal Code 1203.4/1203.4a/1203.41/1203.42] continued to 09/28/2018 at 08:30 AM in Department C53 at request of Defense.**
09/28/18	1	HHELD	**Hearing held on 09/28/2018 at 08:30:00 AM in Department C53 for Motion Dismiss [Penal Code 1203.4/1203.4a/1203.41/1203.42].**
	2	OFJUD	Judicial Officer: Gary M Pohlson, Judge
	3	OFJA	Clerk: N. Robles
	4	OFBAL	Bailiff: E. F. Richardson
	5	OFREP	Court Reporter: Kimberly R Moore
	6	APDDA	People represented by George William McFetridge Jr, Deputy District Attorney, present.
	7	APDWRA	Defendant present in Court with counsel Saif Rahman, Retained Attorney.
	8	CLCON2	**Motion re: Dismiss [Penal Code 1203.4/1203.4a/1203.41/1203.42] continued to 11/02/2018 at 08:30 AM in Department C53 by stipulation of all parties.**
11/02/18	1	HHELD	**Hearing held on 11/02/2018 at 08:30:00 AM in Department C53 for Motion Dismiss [Penal Code 1203.4/1203.4a/1203.41/1203.42].**
	2	OFJUD	Judicial Officer: Gary M Pohlson, Judge
	3	OFJA	Clerk: N. Robles

Name: ▓▓▓▓▓▓▓

Page 42 of 44

MINUTES / ALL CATEGORIES

Case: 06HF2202 F A

2/19/19 2:08 pm

95 | Page

MINUTES

Case : 06HF2202 F A

Name :

Date of Action	Seq Nbr	Code	Text
11/02/18	4	OFBAL	Bailiff: E. F. Richardson
	5	OFREP	Court Reporter: Wendy Tatreau
	6	APDDA	People represented by George William McFetridge Jr, Deputy District Attorney, present.
	7	APNDC	Defendant not present in Court represented by Saif Rahman, Retained Attorney.
	8	CORAC	Court read and considered Petition for Dismissal of case Pursuant to 1203.4.
	9	MOTBY	Oral motion by Defense to withdraw motion.
	10	MOTION	Motion granted.
	11	MOTION	Motion withdrawn.
11/30/18	1	CLADD	**At the request of Defense Counsel, case calendared on 11/30/18 at 08:30 AM in C53 for MTN PC1203.4.**
	2	HHELD	**Hearing held on 11/30/2018 at 08:30:00 AM in Department C53 for Motion Dismiss [Penal Code 1203.4/1203.4a/1203.41/1203.42].**
	3	OFJUD	Judicial Officer: Gary M Pohlson, Judge
	4	OFJA	Clerk: N. Robles
	5	OFBAL	Bailiff: E. F. Richardson
	6	OFREP	Court Reporter: Shelley Hill
	7	APDDA	People represented by George William McFetridge Jr, Deputy District Attorney, present.
	8	APNDC	Defendant not present in Court represented by Saif Rahman, Retained Attorney.
	9	FIMTN	Defense Motion to Dismiss (PC1203.4) filed.
	10	TEXT	Motion Pursuantn to 1473.7 filed in case 07HF0020
	11	CORAC	Court read and considered Motion to Withdraw Plea and Dismiss Case Under Penal Code Section 1203.4.
	12	TRPRS	People submit(s).
	13	MOTION	Motion granted.
	14	FDTXT	Court finds Court finds finds the defendant was not advised of their immigration consequences and grants the motion pursuant to Penal Code 1473.7. The defendant withdraws his guilty plea(s). People state they are unable to proceed at this time. Defense requests the Court dismiss this case in the furtherance of justice. The Court orders this case dismissed pursuant to Penal Code 1385.

MINUTES

Case : 06HF2202 F A

Name : ███████████

Date of Action	Seq Nbr	Code	Text
11/30/18	15	PLWTH	**Defendant's motion to WITHDRAW GUILTY PLEA to count(s) 11, 16, 21, 24, 40, 46, 54 granted.**
	16	CDCDM	Count(s) 11, 16, 21, 24, 40, 46, 54 DISMISSED - pursuant to Penal Code 1385 - Furtherance of justice.
	17	FIORD	Order Vacating Conviction Under Penal Code 1473.7 signed and filed.
02/01/19	1	FXDMVA	Deleted DD1 - Abstract of Conviction abstract from case.

Name: ███████████

Page 44 of 44

MINUTES / ALL CATEGORIES

Case: 06HF2202 F A

2/19/19 2:08 pm

97 | P a g e

EXHIBIT '8':

Respondent's Notice to Appear

U.S. Department of Homeland Security

Notice to Appear

In removal proceedings under section 240 of the Immigration and Nationality Act:

Subject ID : 340760698   FIN #: 1122706063   File No: A████████
                                 DOB: 03/21/1976   Event No: SBD1108000559

In the Matter of:

Respondent: _____ currently residing at:

4500 NORTH 60TH STREET WEST , LANCASTER CALIFORNIA 93536   (661)940-3555

(Number, street, city and ZIP code)   (Area code and phone number)

☐ 1. You are an arriving alien.

☐ 2. You are an alien present in the United States who has not been admitted or paroled.

☒ 3. You have been admitted to the United States, but are removable for the reasons stated below.

The Department of Homeland Security alleges that you:
See Continuation Page Made a Part Hereof

On the basis of the foregoing, it is charged that you are subject to removal from the United States pursuant to the following provision(s) of law:
See Continuation Page Made a Part Hereof

☐ This notice is being issued after an asylum officer has found that the respondent has demonstrated a credible fear of persecution or torture.

☒ Section 235(b)(1) order was vacated pursuant to: ☒ 8CFR 208.30(f)(2) ☐ 8CFR 235.3(b)(5)(iv)

YOU ARE ORDERED to appear before an immigration judge of the United States Department of Justice at:
TO BE DETERMINED

_____
(Complete Address of Immigration Court including Room Number, if any)

on a date to be set at a time to be set to show why you should not be removed from the United States based on the
    (Date)   (Time)
charge(s) set forth above.

Date: 8-26-11   SDDU
                          (Signature and Title of Issuing Officer)

_____
                          (City and State)

See reverse for important information

Form I-862 (Rev. 08/01/07)

Subject ID : 340760698
FINS #: 1122706063

Event No: SBD1108000559
File No: A▓▓▓▓▓▓▓▓▓

Name: ▓▓▓▓▓▓▓▓▓▓▓▓▓▓▓▓▓▓▓▓▓▓▓▓▓▓▓▓▓

NOTICE OF RIGHTS

You have been arrested because immigration officers believe that you are illegally in the United States. You have the right to a hearing before the Immigration Court to determine whether you may remain in the United States. If you request a hearing, you may be detained in custody or you may be eligible to be released on bond, until your hearing date. In the alternative, you may request to return to your country as soon as possible, without a hearing.

You have the right to contact an attorney or other legal representative to represent you at your hearings, or to answer any questions regarding your legal rights in the United States. Upon your request, the officer who gave you this notice will provide you with a list of legal organizations that may represent you for free or for a small fee. You have the right to communicate with the consular or diplomatic officer from your country. You may use a telephone to call a lawyer, other legal representative, or consular officer at any time prior to your departure from the United States.

REQUEST FOR DISPOSITION

☐ I request a hearing before the Immigration Court to determine whether or not I may remain in the
_____ United States.
initials

☒ I believe I face harm if I return to my country. My case will be referred to the Immigration Court
_____ for a hearing.
initials

☒ I admit that I am in the United States illegally, and I believe that I do not face harm if I return to my
_____ country. I give up my right to a hearing before the Immigration Court. I wish to return to my country
initials   as soon as arrangements can be made to effect my departure. I understand that I may be held in
detention until my departure.

_____   _____
Signature of Subject   8-26-11
                                        Date

CERTIFICATION OF SERVICE

☒ Notice read by subject.

☐ Notice read to subject by _____ , in the _____ language.

JAVIER LEMUS
Name of Officer (Print)   Name of Interpreter (Print)

_____   August 26, 2011 12:00 AM
Signature of Officer   Date and Time of Service

Form I-826 (Rev. 08/01/07)

Alien's Name	File Number A043 060 718 Event No: SBD1108000559	Date August 26, 2011
███████████		

OTHER ALIASES KNOWN BY:

███████████ ---

Signature	Title
JAVIER LEMUS	IMMIGRATION ENFORCEMENT AGENT

<u> 2 </u> of <u> 2 </u> Pages

Form I-831 Continuation Page (Rev. 08/01/07)

Alien's Name	File Number	Date
████████	A████████ Event No: SBD1108000559	August 26, 2011

THE SERVICE ALLEGES THAT YOU:
================================
1. You are not a citizen or national of the United States;
2. You are a native of IRAN and a citizen of IRAN;
3. You were admitted to the United States as a Legal Permanent Resident in LOS ANGELES, CALIFORNIA on or about August 29, 1991;
4. You were, on December 11, 2007, convicted in the Superior Court of California county of Orange, Harbor Justice Center for the offense of unauthorized use of personal identification, a felony, in violation of California Penal Code section number 530.5(a).
5. For this offence you were sentences to a period of confinement of two (2) years prison.
6. You were, on or about December 2, 2004 you were convicted in the Superior Court of the state of California county of Orange for Possession of a Controlled Substance, Methamphetamine a felony in violation of Section 11377(a) of the California Health and Safety Code.
7. For this offence you were sentences to a period of confinement of 180 days jail.

ON THE BASIS OF THE FOREGOING, IT IS CHARGED THAT YOU ARE SUBJECT TO REMOVAL FROM THE UNITED STATES PURSUANT TO THE FOLLOWING PROVISION(S) OF LAW:
==

Section 237(a)(2)(A)(iii) of the Immigration and Nationality Act (Act), as amended, in that, at any time after admission, you have been convicted of an aggravated felony as defined in section 101(a)(43)(G) of the Act, a law relating to a theft offense (including receipt of stolen property) or burglary offense for which the term of imprisonment at least 1 year was imposed.

Section 237(a)(2)(B)(i) of the Immigration and Nationality Act, as amended, in that, at any time after admission, you have been convicted of a violation of (or a conspiracy or attempt to violate) any law or regulation of a State, the United States, or a foreign country relating to a controlled substance (as defined in Section 102 of the Controlled Substances Act, 21 U.S.C. 802), other than a single offense involving possession for one's own use of 30 grams or less of marijuana.

Signature	Title
[signature]	SDDO

3 of 3 Pages

Form I-831 Continuation Page (Rev. 08/01/07)

EXHIBIT '9':

Respondent's Order of Supervision

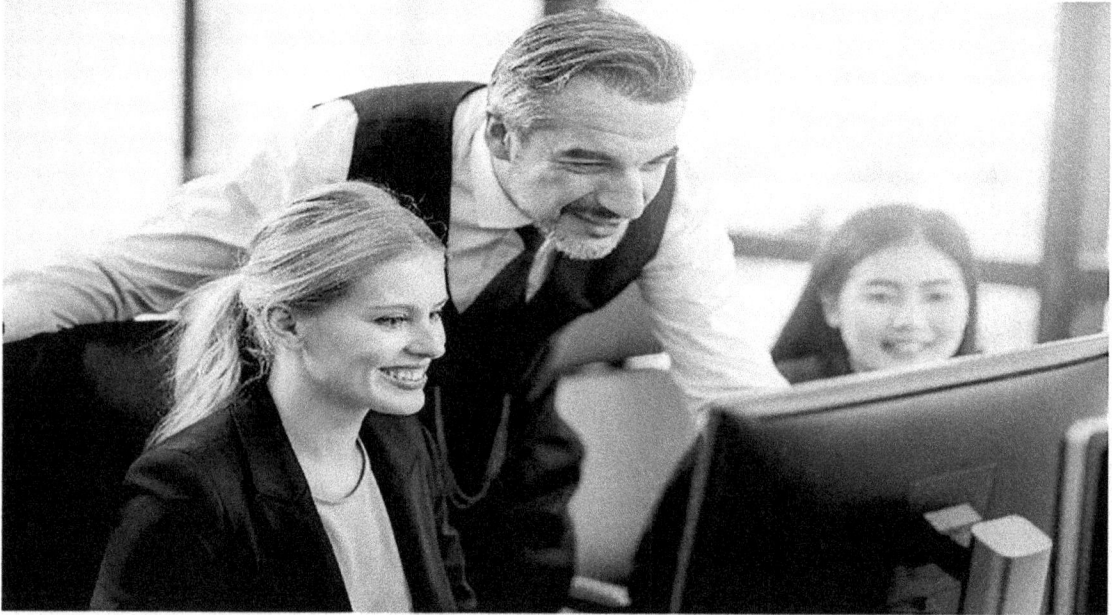

U.S. Department of Homeland Security
U.S. Immigration and Customs Enforcement

Order of Supervision

File No: A43 060 718
Date: 1/23/12

Name: ████████████████

On 1/17/2011 you were ordered:
(Date of final order)

☐ Excluded or deported pursuant to proceedings commenced prior to April 1, 1997.
☒ Removed pursuant to proceedings commenced on or after April 1, 1997.

Because ICE has not effected your deportation or removal during the period prescribed by law, it is ordered that you be placed under supervision and permitted to be at large under the following conditions:

☒ That you appear in person at the time and place specified, upon each and every request of ICE, for identification and for deportation or removal.

☐ That upon request of ICE, you appear for medical or psychiatric examination at the expense of the United States Government.

☒ That you provide information under oath about your nationality, circumstances, habits, associations, and activities and such other information as ICE considers appropriate.

☒ That you do not travel outside _____California_____ for more than 48 hours without first
(Specify geographic limits, if any)
having notified this ICE office of the dates and places of such proposed travel.

☒ That you furnish written notice to this ICE office of any change of residence or employment within 48 hours of such change.

☒ That you report in person, on *February 6, 2012   0900 HRS.* , to the ICE office
300 N. Los Angeles Street, 2nd floor, Room 2204, Los Angeles, Ca. 90012, unless you are granted written permission to report on another date ████████████████████████████████

☒ That you assist U.S. Immigration and Customs Enforcement in obtaining any necessary travel documents.

☒ Other: You shall obey all local, state and federal laws .

☒ See attached sheet containing other specified conditions (Continue on separate sheet if required)

_____T-SRbll_____
62
(Signature of ICE official)

Timothy S. Robbins, Field Office Director
(Print name and title of ICE official)

Alien's Acknowledgment of Conditions of Release under an Order of Supervision

I hereby acknowledge that I have (read) (had interpreted and explained to me in the Creole language) the contents of this order, a copy of which has been given to me. I understand that failure to comply with the terms of this order may subject me to a fine, detention, or prosecution.

Debbie Lemo   X _____   1/23/12
(Signature of ICE official serving order)   (Signature of alien)   Date

U.S. Department of Homeland Security
U.S. Immigration and Customs Enforcement

Continuation Page for Form   I-220B

Alien's Name	File Number	Date
███████████	A ████████	1/23/12

███████████ (redacted)

_ ✗ _K. Hsu_

Alien's Signature

Alien's Address

26702 Aracena Drive

Mission Viejo, CA 92691

949-463-1877

Alien's Telephone Number (if any)

RIGHT INDEX PRINT

PERSONAL REPORT RECORD

DATE	OFFICER	COMMENT/CHANGES
2/6/12	S.C.	R/D RTN: 5/7/12.
5/7/12	JC	(Subject/sup. NNK3 - negative), return) 8/7/12.
8/7/12	JC	Reported in; NNK3 - negative; return) 11/7/12
11/07/12	JY	R/D Return FEB 07 2013
		2/7/14
2/7/13	4	M going to AZ-18/5-14, RTN
2/7/14	W	MB O/sup RTN 2/9/15
02/09/15		RTN 02/09/16
02/09/17		O/sup RTN: 02/09/18
2/9/18	W	TSSup RTN 2/8/19
02/07/19		RTN 02/07/2020

Signature	Title

Order of Supervision

File No: A▮▮▮▮▮
Date: 1/23/12

ame: ▮▮▮▮▮▮▮▮

] That you do not associate with criminals or members of a gang that is known to be involved in criminal ctivity.

] That you register in a substance abuse program within 14 days and provide Immigration and Customs Enforcement (ICE) with written proof of such within 30 days. The proof must include the name, address, duration, and objectives of the program as well as the name of a program counselor.

] That you register in a sexual deviancy counseling program within 14 days and provide ICE with written proof of such within 30 days. You must provide ICE with the name of the program, the address of the program, the duration and objectives of the program, and the name of a program counselor.

☐ That you register as a sex offender, if applicable, within 7 days of being released, with the appropriate agency/agencies and provide ICE with written proof of such registration within 10 days.

☒ That you do not commit any crimes or be associated with any criminal activity while on this Order of Supervision.

☒ That you report to a parole or probation officer as required within 5 business days and provide ICE with written verification of the officer's name, address, telephone number, and reporting requirements.

☒ You must follow all reporting and supervision requirements as mandated by the parole or probation officer.

☐ That you continue to follow any prescribed doctor's orders whether medical or psychological, including taking prescribed medications.

☐ That you make good faith and timely efforts to obtain a travel document and assist ICE in obtaining a travel document.

☐ That you submit a complete application for a travel document to all appropriate Embassies or Consulates, including those representing the countries of <u>IRAN</u>. You must present ICE with evidence that each Embassy or Consulate to which you apply has received your request and all required documents. This may be done, for example, by mailing your application(s) with a request for return receipt and providing the signed return receipt to ICE, by obtaining a tracking number when you mail your application(s) and providing the number to ICE, or by submitting written confirmation of receipt issued by the Embassy or Consulate.

☐ That you submit your application(s) for a travel document to all appropriate Embassies or Consulates and provide proof of receipt to ICE on or before_____.

☐ That you provide ICE a copy of your application(s) for a travel document that you submit to any Embassy or Consulate, including all supporting documents, photos, and other items provided to the Embassy or Consulate to support your application(s).

☐ That you provide ICE a copy of all correspondence related to your travel document application(s) that you send to, or receive from, an Embassy or Consulate.

☐ That you contact the Embassy or Consulate within 21 calendar days of making your application(s) to confirm that the information you provided is sufficient.

☒ That you comply with any requests from an Embassy or Consulate for an interview and make good faith efforts to submit further documentation if required by the Embassy or Consulate.

☒ Every time you report in person under this order of supervision, you must inform the local ICE office of all actions you have taken to obtain a travel document. You must provide any available written documentation to ICE regarding these actions and the status of your travel document application(s).

☐ That you provide ICE, upon request, with any and all information relevant to application(s) for a travel document. This may include, but is not limited to, information regarding your family history, including dates of birth, nationalities, addresses, and phone numbers as requested for such persons, whether in your country of nationality and/or citizenship or elsewhere, and your past residences, schools attended, etc.

☐ You will participate in a supervised release program, as described in the attached document. You will comply with the rules and requirements of this program, and cooperate with its administrators.

I agree to comply with the rules, requirements, and administrators in the supervised release program described in the attached document.

Alien's signature _X K. Ash_____ Date __1/23/12_____

☐ Other. _____

_____

_____

_____

Any violation of any of the above conditions may result in a fine, more restrictive release conditions, return to detention, criminal prosecution, and/or revocation of your employment authorization document.

Alien's Acknowledgement of Conditions of Release under an Order of Supervision

I hereby acknowledge that I have (read) the contents of this order and addendum, a copy of which has been given to me. I understand that failure to comply with the terms of this order and addendum may subject me to a fine, more restrictive release conditions, detention, criminal prosecution, and/or revocation of my employment authorization document.

Debbie Lenz   _K. Ash_   _1/23/12_
(Signature of ICE official serving order)   (Signature of alien)   (Date)

Please note that all references in this order/addendum to "INS" or "Service" should now be considered to refer to U.S. Immigration and Customs Enforcement (ICE).

Updated 4/25/200

AT INDEX.

United States Department of Justice
Executive Office for Immigration Review
Immigration Court
Los Angeles, California

In the Matter of:

███████████████

ORDER OF THE IMMIGRATION JUDGE

Upon consideration of Respondent's Motion to Reopen and Terminate Removal Proceedings Based on Convictions Vacated Pursuant to Section 1473.7 of the California Penal Code, it is HEREBY ORDERED that the motion be [ ] **GRANTED** [ ] **DENIED** because:

    [ ] DHS does not oppose the motion.
    [ ] Respondent does not oppose the motion.
    [ ] A response to the motion has not been filed with the Court.
    [ ] Good case has been established for the motion.
    [ ] The Court agrees with the reasons stated in the opposition to the motion.
    [ ] The motion is untimely per _____.
    [ ] Other:

Deadlines:

    [ ] The application (s) for relief must be filed by _____.
    [ ] Respondent must comply with DHS biometrics instructions by_____.

_____
Date

_____
Kevin W. Riley
Immigration Judge

Certificate of Service
This document was served by: _____ Mail _____ Personal Service
To: [ ] Alien [ ] Alien c/o Custodial Officer [ ] Alien's Atty/Rep [ ] DHS
  Date: _____   By: Court Staff: _____

CERTIFICATE OF SERVICE

Re: ███████████

I, Christopher A. Reed, hereby certify that I am a resident of or employed in the County of Los Angeles, State of California over 18 years of age, not a party to the within action and that I am employed at and my business address is:

Law Offices of Brian D. Lerner, APC
3233 E. Broadway
Long Beach, CA 90803
Telephone: (562) 495-0554
Facsimile: (562) 608-8672

On February 22, 2019, I served a copy of the attached **MOTION TO REOPEN AND TERMINATE REMOVAL PROCEEDINGS BASED ON CONVICTIONS VACATED PURSUANT TO SECTION 1473.7 OF THE CALIFORNIA PENAL CODE** on the following person(s) by the following method(s):

Office of the Assistant Chief Counsel
Department of Homeland Security
300 N. Los Angeles Street, Suite 8108
Los Angeles, CA 90012
(USPS First-Class Mail)

I declare under penalty of perjury that the foregoing is true and correct. Executed in Long Beach, California.

DATED: February 22, 2019

By: _____
Christopher A. Reed
Attorney at Law

ABOUT THE AUTHOR

Brian D. Lerner is an Immigration Lawyer and runs a National Immigration Law Firm for nearly 30 years. He is an attorney who is a certified specialist that might help in Immigration & Nationality Law as issued by the California State Bar, Board of Legal Specialization. Attorney Lerner is an expert in Immigration Law, Removal and Deportation, Citizenship, Waiver and Appeals.

He has been a licensed attorney since 1992 and started the Law Offices of Brian D. Lerner, APC. The immigration practice consists of Immigration and Nationality Law, and everything involved with and regarding immigration which includes citizenship, investment visas, family and employment visas, removal and deportation hearings, appeals, waivers, adjustment, consulate processing and all types of immigration and citizenship matters.

He has represented clients from all over the U.S. and in many countries around the world. One side of his practice is dedicated to keeping people in the U.S. and fighting for their immigration rights, while another side is to get people back who have been deported and removed from the U.S.

Also, there is the affirmative part of Immigration Law which Brian Lerner has helped numerous people come into the U.S. on business visas, investment visas, student visas, fiancée and marriage visas, religious visas and many more. Attorney Lerner has helped immigrants who are victims of crime and domestic violence or ones that are married to abusers.

In other words, Attorney Lerner has a firm that helps people all over the U.S. He has dedicated significant time to preparing numerous petitions and applications for you to get at a fraction of the price of hiring an attorney. He says it is the next best thing to a real attorney because they are real petitions prepared by an expert.